FESTAL ORATIONS

St Gregory of Nazianzus

T0312559

ST VLADIMIR'S SEMINARY PRESS
Popular Patristics Series
Number 36

The Popular Patristics Series published by St Vladimir's Seminary Press provides readable and accurate translations of a wide range of early Christian literature to a wide audience—students of Christian history to lay Christians reading for spiritual benefit. Recognized scholars in their fields provide short but comprehensive and clear introductions to the material. The texts include classics of Christian literature, thematic volumes, collections of homilies, letters on spiritual counsel, and poetical works from a variety of geographical contexts and historical backgrounds. The mission of the series is to mine the riches of the early Church and to make these treasures available to all.

Series Editor
BOGDAN BUCUR

Associate Editor
IGNATIUS GREEN

* * *

Series Editor
1999–2020
JOHN BEHR

Festal Orations

ST GREGORY OF NAZIANZUS

Translation with Introduction
and Commentary by

NONNA VERNA HARRISON

ST VLADIMIR'S SEMINARY PRESS
CRESTWOOD, NEW YORK
2008

Library of Congress Cataloging-in-Publication Data

Gregory of Nazianzus, Saint.
    [Orations. Selections. English]
    Festal orations / St. Gregory of Nazianzus : translation with introduction and
commentary by Nonna Verna Harrison.
        p. cm. — (Popular patristics series, ISSN 1555–5755 ; no. 36)
    Includes bibliographical references.
    ISBN 978–0–88141–325–0 (alk. paper)
    1. Church year sermons. 2. Sermons, Greek—Translations into English.
3. Speeches, addresses, etc., Greek— Translations into English. 4. Orthodox
Eastern Church—Sermons. I. Harrison, Verna E. F. II. Title.

    BR65.G62E5 2008
    252'.6—dc22

                                                            2008045868

COPYRIGHT © 2008
ST VLADIMIR'S SEMINARY PRESS
575 Scarsdale Road, Crestwood, NY 10707
1-800-204-2665
www.svspress.com

ISBN 978–088141–325–0
ISSN 1555–5755

PRINTED IN THE UNITED STATES OF AMERICA

For Fr. Stephan and Matushka Elaine Meholick,

with thanksgiving.

Contents

Preface

I would like to thank the faculty, students, and library staff of Saint Paul School of Theology for their support and encouragement during the writing of this book. Let me also thank the editor, Augustine Casiday, and the staff at St Vladimir's Seminary Press, for their diligent work on the manuscript.

In addition, let me acknowledge with appreciation the publishers of material that is reprinted, with revisions, here. An earlier version of my translation of Oration 38 was published as "Gregory Nazianzen, Homily on the Birth of Christ," in *Religions of Late Antiquity in Practice*, edited by Richard Valantasis and published by Princeton University Press.[1] Material incorporated into this book's Introduction has appeared in "Gregory Nazianzen's Festal Spirituality: Anamnesis and Mimesis," in *Philosophy and Theology*,[2] and also in an article forthcoming in *Studia Patristica*, "The Word Cries Out from the Virgin's Womb: Gregory of Nazianzus, *Oration* 45.13."[3]

I have endeavored to convey the beauty of Gregory's rhetorical prose as far as is possible in clear, contemporary English. Inevitably, I have fallen short. This gap between text and translation, and any other errors that may be found in this book, are my responsibility.

---

[1] N.V. Harrison, "Gregory Nazianzen, Homily on the Birth of Christ," in *Religions of Late Antiquity in Practice* (ed. Richard Valantasis; Princeton, NJ: Princeton University Press, 2000).

[2] N.V. Harrison, "Gregory Nazianzen's Festal Spirituality: Anamnesis and Mimesis," *Philosophy and Theology* 18 (2006): 27–51.

[3] N.V. Harrison, "The Word Cries Out from the Virgin's Womb: Gregory of Nazianzus, *Oration* 45.13," *Studia Patristica*, forthcoming.

Introduction

In the Orthodox church Gregory of Nazianzus (ca. AD 329–ca. 390) is known as "the Theologian," a title he shares only with the apostle and evangelist John, and is among the most honored of the saints. Together with his colleagues Basil the Great (ca. 329–379) and Gregory of Nyssa (ca. 335–395), he is one of the three Cappadocian fathers, and together with Basil and John Chrysostom (ca. 347–407) he is one of the "three great hierarchs and ecumenical teachers" of the Eastern church. His reputation and influence in the Byzantine world as both theologian and rhetor are unsurpassed in ways that Western scholars have sometimes overlooked. The homilies translated in this volume have arguably been the most influential of his works throughout the Orthodox church's history.

Byzantines made more copies of Gregory's writings than of any other texts except those of Holy Scripture. His theological influence was pervasive in the eastern Roman world. Maximus the Confessor's *Ambigua* is a commentary on difficult passages in his orations, and twenty other Byzantine commentaries or scholia on his works are known.[1] Rufinus translated nine of his orations into Latin in about 400, and there are also ancient or medieval translations in Armenian, Syriac, Slavonic, Coptic, Georgian, Arabic and Ethiopic.[2]

The Theologian was read for the content of what he said, but just as much for the beautiful ways he said it. George A. Kennedy observes that "Gregory became the great model for the union of Greek eloquence and Christianity and was so studied throughout

[1]John Behr, *The Nicene Faith* (2 vols.; Crestwood, NY: SVS Press, 2004), 2:331–332.
[2]George A. Kennedy, *Greek Rhetoric under Christian Emperors* (Princeton, NJ: Princeton University Press, 1983), 239.

11

the Byzantine period."[3] In a culture that prized rhetoric as a privi-
leged form of artistic expression, Gregory's orations were read in the
rhetorical classroom as well as in the theologian's study. In middle
Byzantine commentaries on the classical textbooks of rhetoric,
examples from Gregory's writings came to replace those gathered
in earlier centuries from the pagan classical orators. Leading men of
letters praised his literary style above that of Demosthenes.[4] His style
was imitated to such an extent that phrases from his writings turn
up without attribution in unexpected places throughout Byzantine
literature.[5]

Gregory's homilies were also appointed for reading in church. By
the ninth century, sixteen of his forty-five orations had been chosen
to be read on specific feast days or saint's days, or as commentary
on the gospel lesson for the day. At least thirty-four manuscripts of
all or part of this subset are extant, some of them beautifully illu-
minated, in which the order of the homilies follows the lectionary
and the liturgical calendar.[6] The orations on Pascha, Christ's Nativity, Theophany, Holy Baptism, and Pentecost, translated here, are
prominent on the list. Their reading at the high points of the church
year must have brought them to large audiences. Two overlapping
collections of Gregory's orations, one with thirteen homilies and one
with sixteen, were translated into Slavonic in tenth-century Bulgaria
for reading in church or in the monastic refectory, and passed from
there into the Russian Orthodox tradition.[7]

---

[3]Kennedy, *Greek Rhetoric*, 238.

[4]Behr, *The Nicene Faith*, 2:331; Kennedy, *Greek Rhetoric*, 238; George L. Kustas,
Studies in Byzantine Rhetoric (Thessaloniki: Analecta Vlatadon, 1973), 21, 24–25.

[5]Jacques Noret, "Grégoire de Nazianze, l'auteur le plus cité, après la Bible, dans la
littérature ecclésiastique byzantine," in *Symposium Nazianzenum, Louvain-la-Neuve,
25–28 août 1981* (ed. Justin Mossay; Paderborn: Ferdinand Schöningh, 1983), 259–66.

[6]George Galavaris, *The Illustrations of the Liturgical Homilies of Gregory Nazianzenus* (Princeton, NJ: Princeton University Press, 1969), 6–17. The homilies read
liturgically are listed below in the Appendix together with their appointed dates in
the Byzantine church calendar.

[7]Francis J. Thomson, *The Reception of Byzantine Culture in Mediaeval Russia*
(Aldershot, UK: Ashgate Variorum, 1999), I:108–110. One Slavonic collection contains Orations 1–2, 5–6, 16, 27–28, 38–41, 43 and 45. The other contains Orations 1,

Moreover, the poetic prose of Gregory's homilies, especially the *Festal Orations*, is quoted extensively in Byzantine hymnography,[8] often in texts that are still sung in Byzantine rite churches today. Some medieval Western hymns quote Gregory as well.[9] John of Damascus, a patristic scholar as well as a poet, drew heavily from the Theologian, as did other hymnographers. Andrew Louth has shown how the Damascene used Gregory's orations as his primary source in composing the Paschal Canon,[10] which is sung at the high point of the church year. So Orthodox Christians have been learning and praying his theology in church for over a thousand years, even if they have never read his writings. Attentive readers familiar with the church's festal hymnography will find passages in this book that seem strikingly familiar.

In the West, Gregory is best known for his *Five Theological Orations*, a classic response to the theology of Eunomius, a late, radicalized form of Arianism.[11] However, the opinion of some scholars that he would have been a minor figure had he not written the *Theological Orations* ignores the vast range of his impact in the Eastern churches, where his *Festal Orations* have been a formative influence. In the context of festal proclamation and celebration Gregory articulates his own theology with emphases and rhetorical features different from those found in the five discourses where he debates his neo-Arian opponents on their own ground. He also shows clearly how the doctrines he proclaims are inseparably intertwined with his

---

16, 38–41, 43 and 45, found in the first collection, plus Orations 11, 14–15, 19, 21, 24, 42 and 44.

[8]Behr, *The Nicene Faith*, 2:331; Peter Karavites, "Gregory Nazianzinos and Byzantine Hymnography," *Journal of Hellenic Studies* 113 (1993): 81–98.

[9]Peter Jeffery, "Παράδοξον Μυστύριον: The Thought of Gregory the Theologian in Byzantine and Latin Liturgical Chant," *Greek Orthodox Theological Review* 39 (1994): 187–98.

[10]Andrew Louth, *St John Damascene: Tradition and Originality in Byzantine Theology* (Oxford: Oxford University Press, 2002), 258–274.

[11]On Eunomius and his place in the controversies about Arius, see now Richard P. Vaggione, *Eunomius of Cyzicus and the Nicene Revolution* (Oxford: Oxford University Press, 2000).

pastoral teachings about Christian life. These homilies' distinctive festal emphases have contributed to the shaping of Eastern Christian theology and spirituality in ways that have escaped the notice of those who read only the *Theological Orations*, as important as they truly are.

Gregory's Life and Work

Gregory was born near Nazianzus in Cappadocia of a wealthy aristocratic family.[12] His father, a distinguished landowner and civic leader known to posterity as Gregory the Elder, belonged to a religious group that worshipped the "Most High God," but in middle age he converted to Christianity through the influence of his wife Nonna, a devout lifelong Christian, and soon became pastor of his local community. He served as bishop of Nazianzus for about fifty years and built a church there. He and Nonna had three children, a daughter Gorgonia and two sons, Gregory and his younger brother Caesarius. The younger Gregory remained close to his family and wrote about them. All five are considered saints in the Orthodox world.

Gregory the Elder sent both sons abroad to obtain the best higher education available in the fourth-century Roman world. In 347–348 they went first to Caesarea in Palestine where Origen had taught in the previous century and where his library and teachings remained an active presence, and then to Origen's home town, Alexandria, a multicultural center of philosophical, Jewish and Christian learning. Gregory probably learned some of the rich heritage of theology, biblical interpretation and spiritual life from Christian

[12]On Gregory's life and work, Brian E. Daley's superb introduction in *Gregory of Nazianzus* (London and New York: Routledge, 2006), 1–61, is a good starting point. For a more extensive study, see John McGuckin, *Saint Gregory of Nazianzus: An Intellectual Biography* (Crestwood, NY: SVS Press, 2001). Daley, 266, remarks judiciously that McGuckin's volume is "the fullest and most recent study of Gregory's life. Learned, detailed, sometimes speculative, always thoughtful and readable."

teachers in both these cities. Caesarius, who later served as a physician at the imperial court in Constantinople, stayed in Alexandria to study medicine, but in 348 Gregory moved on to Athens, which in this period was an ancient and international university town, rather like Oxford or Cambridge today. Students went there from around the Mediterranean world to immerse themselves in Greek classical culture. Gregory fell in love with the scholarly life there and stayed for ten years of graduate work in rhetoric, the art of education and advocacy, of finely crafted writing and public speaking. Its study also involved learning philosophy, classical literature, and literary criticism. In Athens Gregory roomed with Basil, a fellow Cappadocian student and close friend. Both excelled in their studies, were devoted to the church, and vowed to dedicate their lives to God's service. When Basil left to go home to Cappadocia, Gregory stayed on for another year. He may have begun teaching in Athens and perhaps was offered a faculty position there, but he too returned home in 358 or 359. His extensive education would prove invaluable in his subsequent work as pastor, preacher, theologian, and poet.

Between 358 or 359 and 361, Gregory lived in semi-seclusion with his family in Nazianzus. He may have taught rhetoric briefly, and from time to time he visited Basil at the monastic community he had founded in Pontus. At the end of 361 his father ordained him priest against his will. He immediately went to Pontus for several months' retreat and study with Basil, then returned and accepted his pastoral duties at Pascha in 362. At that feast he preached his first sermon, Oration 1, which celebrates Christ's resurrection, cements his reconciliation with his father and the congregation, and already articulates major themes in Gregory's theology and spirituality. He would serve as a pastor, preacher and teacher for the rest of his life, sometimes in direct ministry to congregations and sometimes from a distance through writing. His work as priest and bishop proved effective and influential, at least in the long run, though during his lifetime he had a checkered career. His discernment and sensitive appreciation of those close to him made him a loving and beloved pastor, especially in small congregations, but he would have more difficulty with large congregations such as the city of Constantinople. His ideal of Christian perfection was a balance between action and contemplation. He sought to embody this ideal by alternating between periods of active ministry and solitary, prayerful, scholarly contemplation.

From 362 to 372 Gregory served as a priest assisting his father in Nazianzus. In 372 Basil, who had become archbishop of Caesarea in Cappadocia, ordained Gregory bishop of Sasima, a small town that was disputed between Basil and another metropolitan bishop. Gregory was upset with this appointment, which was apparently motivated by issues of power politics, and never went to Sasima, perhaps because people there would not have accepted him. He returned instead to Nazianzus and again assisted his elderly father, but he and Basil were never fully reconciled during their lifetime. After his parents both died in 374 he went to Seleucia to live a monastic life near a large convent dedicated to St Thecla, the companion of St Paul and first woman martyr. He devoted himself to prayer, silence, and probably study and spiritual direction.

In 378, when Theodosius, who supported the Nicene faith, had become emperor of the East as well as the West, and all the churches in Constantinople remained in the hands of various kinds of "Arians," Gregory was invited to go as a missionary bishop to strengthen the small struggling Nicene community in the capital. As a learned and eloquent bishop free from other pastoral responsibilities, he was well qualified for this challenging assignment. His ministry in Constantinople lasted only from 379 to 381, but his work there was intense and brilliant. It came at a major turning point in church history; Gregory was well aware of this fact and was a major player in bringing about the transformation. Many of his most important orations date from this brief period. When he arrived, he stayed with a wealthy cousin and established a chapel in her home dedicated to the resurrection. He preached to everyone who came, both supporters and opponents, including members of the urban aristocracy. Many came to hear his splendid oratory, and he persuaded some to accept his Orthodox theology. There in 380 he preached Oration 41 at Pentecost. During that summer he presented his famous *Five Theological Orations*, in which he argued for the full divinity of the Son and the Holy Spirit against the followers of Eunomius.

On November 27, the day after his arrival in the city, the emperor Theodosius installed Gregory in the cathedral of the Holy Apostles as archbishop of Constantinople and put him in charge of all the churches in the city. It was an astonishing turnaround, though Gregory was not well prepared for the administrative responsibilities and political hardball that accompanied his new position. He presented his faith in the cathedral in a series of three festal orations (38–40), at Christmas in 380 and at Epiphany and the next day in 381. From May to July of that year he took part in the Council of Constantinople, which Theodosius convened to re-establish the Nicene Creed and clarify the church's teaching about the Holy Spirit. Due to theological and political disputes in the council, Gregory was pressured into resignation. He returned to Cappadocia before the council was finished.

The see in Nazianzus was still vacant, so Gregory again assumed episcopal responsibilities there until his retirement in 383. During this time he preached Oration 45, *On Pascha*.[13] After his retirement he continued to teach and advocate for Orthodox theology in writing. He sent letters to influential people, edited collections of his letters and orations, and wrote many poems, some theological, some devoted to moral instruction, and some autobiographical. His influential writings persuaded the church to understand the Creed of Constantinople, which is the version of the Nicene Creed used in churches to this day, as unequivocally affirming the full divinity of the Holy Spirit.

[13]He preached one other festal oration, Oration 44, *On New Sunday*, that is, the first Sunday after Pascha. Daley, 155, has argued that it dates from the early 370s. Since two modern English translations of this oration have recently appeared, it is not included in this volume. See Martha Vinson, trans., *St Gregory of Nazianzus: Select Orations*, Fathers of the Church 107 (Washington, DC: Catholic University of America Press, 2003), 230–38; and Daley, 155–61. Of the two, Daley's rendering is preferable.

Emergence of the Feast Days

What feast days was Gregory celebrating? It turns out that this is not an easy question, given that he lived in an age of rapid liturgical development, just as it was also an age of rapid doctrinal development. One wonders whether the new prominence of Christmas as the feast of Christ's nativity and Pentecost as the feast of the Holy Spirit were attempts to support the full divinity of the Son and Spirit in controversy? Perhaps liturgical developments were more organic and less calculated than that. Yet Gregory certainly took advantage of the feasts to advocate for his theological agenda from the pulpit.

The first Christian feast was Pascha, which was clearly eschatological; by one great event it transferred the congregation from this world into the new age of the resurrection, there to meet the Risen Lord. Every Sunday, too, was a little Pascha. However, as time went on, two festal cycles emerged and between them came to structure the liturgical year, that of Christ's birth and that of his death and resurrection. Pascha grew into Holy Week, was preceded by Lent and followed by Pentecost; the once central event came to unfold over time and sanctify temporal life. Some earlier liturgical scholars therefore came to contrast the eschatological and the temporal, as if the Church traded its fervor for the life to come for the structuring of time in this world. Yet a more recent scholar, Robert Taft, observes that detailed historical study does not support this thesis; rather, "the history of liturgy and its mystagogy has not progressed in any organic evolution from 'pre-Nicene eschatology' to 'Constantinian historicism.'"[14] Gregory's texts show awareness of both the structuring and sanctification of time and a deep longing for the eschaton. The two intentions need not be mutually exclusive.

A related problem is whether the feasts look toward the past, the time when the events being celebrated took place, or the future, the age to come. Again, Gregory's texts do both and show that this

[14]Robert Taft, "Historicism Revisited," in *idem, Beyond East & West: Problems in Liturgical Understanding* (Washington, DC: Pastoral Press, 1984), 14–30, at 23.

question is a false dichotomy. Indeed, the feasts proclaim Christ's presence here and now. As another liturgical scholar, Thomas J. Talley, observes, it is characteristic of Christian existence as such to live between Christ's coming in the incarnation and his coming at the close of the present age:

> We always live, this is to say, between memory and hope, between his coming and his coming; and the present which is the threshold between these, between memory and hope, between past and future, this present is the locus of the presence of him who is at once Lord of history and its consummation. The remembrance of his passion and the recognition of his glory are integral to one another, and have been from the beginning.[15]

Talley eloquently describes the space in which the feasts, and all of our present life, take place.

> In Gregory's time there were regional variations in festal celebration. The patterns occurring in Rome, Antioch, or Egypt were in flux and may have differed from what occurred at Constantinople. There is not enough historical evidence to provide a definitive map of what was celebrated where, and when. It is clear that as Holy Week looked forward to Christ's resurrection, Pascha looked back and reflected on his passion. These concerns need not be mutually exclusive in order to extend the celebration from one day into Good Friday and Pascha. The same focus on the passion occurs in Gregory's Paschal orations, especially Or. 45 with its extensive meditation on the Paschal lamb. In addition, although Pentecost originally marked the close of fifty days of Paschal

---

[15]Thomas J. Talley, "History and Eschatology in the Primitive Pascha," in Maxwell E. Johnson, ed., *Between Memory and Hope: Readings on the Liturgical Year* (Collegeville, MN: Liturgical Press, 2000), 99–109, at 109.

celebration, it had come in Gregory's time to be a feast of the Holy Spirit, as we see in Or. 41.[16]

The date of Christmas has been debated extensively. Its celebration on December 25 originated in the West and then spread to the East. It was introduced in Constantinople very shortly before Gregory's time, so he explains what it means:

Now is the feast of the Theophany, and so also of the Nativity; for it is called both, since two names are ascribed to one reality. For God appeared to human beings through birth. On the one hand he is and is eternally from the eternal Being, above cause and principle, for there was no principle higher than the Principle. On the other hand for us he later comes into being, that the one who has given us being might also grant us well-being; or rather that, as we fell from well-being through evil, he might bring us back again to himself through incarnation. The name is Theophany, since he has appeared, and Nativity, since he has been born (Oration 38.3).

To avoid confusion, Oration 38, originally called *On the Theophany*, is called *On the Nativity* in this book, since Gregory here gives it both names. Likewise, we have renamed Oration 39, *On the Holy Lights*, as *On the Baptism of Christ*. This shifting of names marks the reorganization of festal dates that was taking place in Constantinople at the time.

In the East the feast of Epiphany, January 6, originally included Christ's birth, the adoration of the magi, and Christ's baptism, a pattern that survives in the Armenian Church to the present. So McGuckin argues that Oration 38 was preached one day before Oration 39.[17] Yet I would disagree with him for three reasons. (1) As with

---

[16]For extensive study of the church year, its regional variations and developments over time, see Thomas J. Talley, *The Origins of the Liturgical Year* (2d ed.; Collegeville, MN: Liturgical Press, 1986).

[17]McGuckin, *Saint Gregory of Nazianzus*, 338–341.

Pascha, there was a trend toward differentiation; an all-inclusive feast became a cycle that unfolds over time. Although it is clear that Orations 38, 39, and 40 were a sermon series, surely the congregation could remember what so eloquent a preacher had said twelve days before. So Oration 38 need not have been presented the day before Oration 39. (2) There is no historical evidence of how Christmas would make a quick transition to Theophany from morning to evening of one day. (3) Why would Gregory spend so long on January 6 cleansing the feast from pagan associations (Oration 39.3–7) if his audience had been in church the day before?

The question of the date of Christmas is difficult. Taft cites Talley as observing that "we have what appears to be a back-and-forth Constantinopolitan pattern"; in 602, Christ's nativity is again celebrated there on January 6. Taft then refers to "quicksands" and a "quagmire" regarding this question.[18] Susan K. Roll, the most recent scholar to study the question, cites numerous scholars on both sides.[19] Taft is the leading specialist in Byzantine liturgics, and Talley is the leader in tracing the evolution of the early church calendar. I cannot say that I can know better than either of them, but I believe Gregory's texts support December 25.

Rhetoric and Liturgy

The Theologian remained devoted to Greek culture, language and eloquence all his life, yet he transformed the rhetoric he had learned into a sacred art by dedicating it to the Holy Trinity as an instrument of praise and proclamation. Late in his pastoral career, at Pascha in Nazianzus, he observes that nobody can celebrate the feast worthily, not even the angels, but exhorts each to offer a festal gift to God as

[18]Robert Taft, "The Beginning, the End, and What Happens in Between: The Origins and Meaning of the Liturgical Year, Apropos of a Recent Book," *Orientalia Christiana Periodica* 52 (1991): 409–415, at 413. He reviews Talley, cited in n. 15, above.

[19]Susan K. Roll, *Toward the Origins of Christmas* (Kampen, The Netherlands: Kak Pharos, 1995), 192.

he or she is able. As he has done since his youth, Gregory offers the one possession he values most, his eloquence: "We will contribute a discourse, the most beautiful and most honorable thing we have, especially when singing the praises of the Word for a good deed done for reason-endowed nature" (Oration 45.2). In this sentence, the orator brings together three meanings of the Greek word λόγος: (1) it is a proper name of *God the Word*, the second person of the Trinity, to whom the feast is dedicated; (2) it also names the *rationality* of human beings made in God's image, including the preacher and his audience who have received Christ's gift of new life and at the feast offer thanks in return; and (3) the *discourse* itself, the finely wrought hymnic prose and its solemn oral presentation as the centerpiece of the feast's liturgical celebration. In Gregory's thought, these and other related meanings of λόγος are inextricably woven together. His words of proclamation and praise have become sacred because they speak forth both the divine Word and the human gift of reasoned speech that manifests God's image and likeness. In his Christmas homily at Constantinople he observes that in contrast to the excesses common at winter holidays, a discourse is the best way to celebrate the feast: "If we, for whom the Word is an object of worship, must somehow have luxury, let us have as our luxury the word and the divine law and narratives, especially those that form the basis of the present feast, that our luxury may be akin and not foreign to the one who has called us" (Oration 38.6). In this sentence λόγος refers to the divine person, the word of Scripture that has been read, and Gregory's festal discourse.

All of Gregory's works are written in traditional Greek literary styles and genres: orations, letters and poems. He has mastered the classical forms and uses them in creative, innovative ways. George A. Kennedy remarks that his *Festal Orations* are "a uniquely Christian form of panegyric"; they celebrate the major Christian feasts and lack classical allusions but abound in biblical allusions instead.[20] Gregory often creates exquisitely detailed tapestries of biblical

[20]Kennedy, *Greek Rhetoric*, 238.

allusions rather than employing direct quotations. Frances Young explains that such a piling up of words and phrases from canonical texts is standard in classical panegyric. In Christian rhetoric it becomes a distinct way of incorporating Scripture that differs from allegory and support for logical argumentation, though Gregory employs biblical texts in these ways too. The "elaborate collages" of allusions are not mere ornament but add weight, authority and content to Gregory's discourse and reveal a creative intertextuality that uses biblical imagery in new ways.[21]

As a pastor and preacher, Gregory uses the words, concepts, images and stories of Scripture to bring the word of God to his audience in their distinctive situation and context. On the feast days the whole church community gathers for common worship to celebrate and praise God's mighty and saving works in the incarnation, baptism, cross and resurrection of Jesus Christ and the descent of the Holy Spirit. Gregory's festal homilies teach doctrine, retell the stories of the events being celebrated, and exhort his hearers to follow the examples of biblical characters who take part in the events. All these dimensions of his preaching invite the congregation to keep the feast authentically.

Gregory considers belief in Orthodox doctrine to be crucially important, and he finds many opportunities to teach it to his audiences. For him doctrinal truth and holiness of life belong together as inseparable dimensions of the journey to God's eternal kingdom. When preaching he often discusses Christology, soteriology and theological anthropology, and in almost every sermon he at least mentions the teaching about the Trinity that forms the heart of his personal spirituality and of his life's work. We will examine his theology below.

Besides providing instruction, his doctrinal proclamation is doxological and enables anamnesis. That is, it makes present what it proclaims. By recounting who God is and what God has done,

[21]Frances M. Young, "Panegyric and the Bible," *Studia Patristica* 25 (1993): 194–208.

Gregory glorifies the One who is present and active at all times and invokes his active, saving and sanctifying presence especially in the festal assembly. In his homily on Christ's birth and again in his second homily on Pascha, he provides a systematic theology in a nutshell.[22] He places himself and his audience within the narrative of all that God has done, is doing and will do in history and thus locates the assembled worshipers within the living stream of salvation history itself. In this context the congregation celebrates Christ's incarnation and resurrection, two central turning points in God's history that are made present in the feasts. Gregory makes explicit this location of the festal congregation within salvation history in Oration 45.1, where an angelic voice proclaims the saving paschal event as present reality and exhorts the faithful to put aside the old Adam in themselves, and be freed from sin and created anew in the risen Christ. This means that through active, freely chosen participation in the pivotal event made present in the feast, people can be transformed by sharing in the salvific outcome of that event.

Festal Anamnesis

Together with readings of biblical texts that tell of the events celebrated, the singing of psalms or hymns praising them, and appropriate prayers, rituals and sacraments,[23] Gregory's homiletic re-tellings and explanations of the festal events enact their anamnesis in liturgical celebration. Anamnesis means re-presentation of God's saving works so that the worshipers can participate in these events as present realities and thereby receive the eschatological salvation, new life

[22]Oration 38.7–13, 45.3–9. At Pascha in Nazianzus Gregory repeats verbatim the same words he spoke at Christmas in Constantinople. This is not the only time he has re-used good material in a new context.

[23]There is little historical evidence about the specific readings, psalms and perhaps hymns, prayers and rituals in Gregory's services. Yet clearly these practices in some form were integral to the festal celebrations. Some information, particularly about his lectionary, can undoubtedly be inferred from the sermons themselves.

and sanctification divinely accomplished through them. Anamnesis thus unites past, present and future in a single present event of worship. Gregory proclaims the past saving events as present and invites his hearers to share in them:

> Christ is born, give glory; Christ is from the heavens, go to meet him; Christ is on earth, be lifted up. "Sing to the Lord, all the earth," and, to say both together, "Let the heavens be glad and let the earth rejoice," for the heavenly one is now earthly (Oration 38.1).

> Christ is illumined,[24] let us flash like lightning with him. Christ is baptized, let us go down with him [into the water], that we may also come up again with him (Oration 39.14).

> Today salvation has come to the world, to things visible and to things invisible. Christ is risen from the dead; rise with him. Christ has returned to himself; return. Christ is freed from the tomb; be freed from the bonds of sin. The gates of hades are opened, and death is destroyed (Oration 45.1).

Anamnesis is historical but is not primarily looking back to the past. Festal celebration is not nostalgia, it is not a commemoration of what once took place but is now present only as a memory, a mere mental phenomenon that the worshipers work to reinforce in order to preserve it from oblivion. Rather, anamnesis is an encounter in the present with the Lord who transfigures and transcends history, and thus it is also a proleptic anticipation of the age to come.[25] Yet

[24]In the early church, "illumination" was another name for baptism, a practice reflected today in Byzantine liturgical practice when it is called "Holy Illumination." In Oration 39, Gregory makes the point that the illumination of Christ, who is himself the Light of the World, is one of the many paradoxes of the incarnation.

[25]Thomas J. Talley, "History and Eschatology in the Primitive Pascha," in his *Worship Reforming Tradition* (Washington, DC: Pastoral Press, 1990), 75–86; Taft, "Historicism Revisited," 15–30.

it is important to note that the saving *events* are made present in their liturgical celebration, not only the persons who once participated in those events and are now glorified in heaven.[26] Since God's saving actions transcend the limitations of temporal sequence, the historical events in which God has acted can be present now and in the future. They are available to us as new beginnings from which a new creation comes forth and grows through time to its consummation in the age to come. So when we participate in these events liturgically and follow their patterns in our own lives, we walk on established paths that lead to God's eternal kingdom. Our personal stories are thereby incorporated into Christ's own story. "Yesterday I was crucified with Christ," Gregory proclaims at his first Pascha as a priest, which is also his homecoming after a time of intense spiritual struggle, "today I am glorified with him; yesterday I died with him, today I am made alive with him; yesterday I was buried with him, today I rise with him" (Oration 1.4). Note this text's double meaning. The festal celebration of the paschal mystery is not isolated from other ways of sharing in Christ's suffering, death and resurrection. Gregory's own life story has followed the same pattern, and he offers his experience to his hearers as an example. To keep the feasts authentically is thus to incorporate the saving events into our core identity and way of life.

In festal celebration the boundaries of sequential time are transcended as the original saving events and the present experience of the congregation join together. The past events of Christ's incarnate life and the Spirit's descent, the present experience of the Christian community, and the future participation in God's kingdom are made one. The joy of the feast is a participation in Paradise restored. The transcendence of temporal boundaries also brings a transcendence of cosmic boundaries as the human worshipers join the angels in their

[26]For a critique of Adolf Adam, *The Liturgical Year*, 21, and Robert Taft, "What Does Liturgy Do?" *Worship* 66:3 (1992): 199–200, see my "Gregory of Nazianzus' Festal Orations: Anamnesis and Mimesis," *Journal of Philosophy and Theology* 18 (2006): 27–51.

witness, awe, praise and hymnody. In this context the worshipers are invited to an encounter with Christ that is both communal and deeply personal, an encounter that brings grace, joy, and salvation.

Gregory understands this festal encounter not as a momentary tasting of a static eternity but as a dynamic interaction in which God comes to meet the faithful as Savior and they come to him in worship and self-offering. The text from Oration 1 quoted above continues with this theme.

> Perhaps you think I am speaking of gold or silver or tapestries or transparent precious stones, earthly matter that is in flux and remains below, of which the greater part belongs to evil people and slaves of things below and of the ruler of this world [John 14.30]. Let us offer our own selves, the possession most precious to God and closest to him. Let us give back to the Image [that is, Christ] that which is according to the image, recognizing our value, honoring the Archetype, knowing the power of the mystery and for whom Christ died (Oration 1.5).

Here the orator reminds his congregation of their great dignity and vocation as human beings which Christ has restored through his death and resurrection and invites them to respond to God's love by offering themselves in return.

The feast is a place of mutual encounter and interchange of gifts between God and his people in which God always gives himself first. According to Gregory, when people choose to make the festal response of self-offering, their task is to transform their whole way of life. In Oration 1, which sought to heal a conflict in Gregory's home congregation, this transformation meant first following Christ's teaching of mutual forgiveness.

> It is the day of resurrection and an auspicious beginning. Let us be made brilliant by the feast and embrace each other. Let

us call brothers even those who hate us [Isa 66.5], and much
more those who have done or suffered anything out of love
for us. Let us concede all things to the resurrection. Let us
grant pardon to each other (Oration 1.1).

Christ's Passover through death to eternal life is present in the
festal celebration as the beginning of a new creation. Yet the feast can
and should continue after the liturgical event concludes. To appropriate and sustain their participation in the new mode of existence
that is risen life in Christ, the worshipers have to change their old
ways of living and relating to one another. Gregory invites them to
begin their community life anew through a reconciliation that honors the resurrection and is enabled by it.

However, besides encountering Christ in festal celebration by
sharing in their worship, the faithful encounter those who were
present with Christ in the events being celebrated. At Epiphany,
Gregory reminds his audience of how they recently celebrated
Christmas: "Therefore at his birth we kept festival, both I the leader
of the feast, and you, and all that is in the world and above the world.
With the star we ran, and with the magi we worshipped, and with
the shepherds we were surrounded by light, and with the angels we
gave glory" (Oration 39.14). At Christmas he invited the faithful to
join the magi, shepherds, and angels in a common act of worship
celebrating the birth of God incarnate: "Run after the star, and bring
gifts with the magi, gold and frankincense and myrrh, as to a king
and a God and one dead for your sake. With the shepherds give
glory, with the angels sing hymns, with the archangels dance. Let
there be a common celebration of the heavenly and earthly powers" (Oration 38.17). Notice how the shared festal worship extends
far beyond the human characters in the biblical nativity stories.
It includes the angels, encompasses the whole cosmos, and unites
heaven and earth. The festal worshipers share in this unity, which
anticipates the eschaton.

Festal Mimesis

As understood by classicists and patristic scholars, mimesis names a pattern of thought and behavior that permeated ancient Mediterranean culture, in which people sought to represent, imitate and identify themselves with exemplary figures from the past. For example, educated late antique men studied and attempted to model themselves upon the heroes of ancient Homeric epic or the philosophers or orators of classical Athens. Mimesis was as foundational for early Christians as it was for their Greco-Roman and Jewish neighbors. Christian models included biblical heroes, martyrs, desert holy men and women, and ultimately Christ himself.[27] Gregory's festal theology and spirituality involve mimesis is several ways, some of which we have already discussed. The liturgical re-presentation of God's saving events in the incarnation and the coming of the Spirit is a mimetic practice. Anamnesis itself is in this sense profoundly mimetic. Baptism, as Gregory shows in Orations 39 and 40, is a re-presentation, imitation of, and participation in Christ's baptism in the Jordan, and also in the death that Jesus names as his "baptism" (Mark 10.38) together with his resurrection. At Theophany, Gregory exhorts the many adult catechumens in his flock to keep the feast by being baptized and invites the faithful to be renewed by the feast in baptismal grace they have received. He says little about the Eucharist because the Cappadocians still observed the traditional *disciplina arcana*; they seldom spoke publicly or wrote about this mystery. Yet obviously the Eucharist is a mimesis of Christ's offering of himself to his disciples at the Last Supper. Moreover, when festal worshipers liturgically re-present, imitate and share in the praise of such figures as the shepherds, magi and angels, again they are practicing mimesis.

[27]On early Christian mimesis, see Peter Brown, "The Saint as Exemplar in Late Antiquity," in J.S. Hawley, ed., *Saints and Virtues* (Berkeley: University of California Press, 1987), 3–14; Derek Krueger, *Writing and Holiness: The Practice of Authorship in the Early Christian East* (Philadelphia: University of Pennsylvania Press, 2004), 15–32; Frances Young, "Panegyric"; and *eadem, Biblical Exegesis and the Formation of Christian Culture* (Cambridge, England: Cambridge University Press, 1997).

Early Christian biblical interpreters such as Gregory found typological links that joined events in Hebrew Scriptures with those in the New Testament and connected both with occurrences in the present lives of believers. This interpretive process draws the church community into a biblical world where all persons and events are linked together through a dense web of mimetic associations. Yet participation in this transhistorical communion is not an automatic absorption of believers' present life and identity into the biblical world but is a matter of free choice. In festal celebration the congregation and the angels and biblical saints meet each other and interact as persons in a free encounter. Gregory's repeated exhortations show that the worshipers are agents who must choose again and again to participate in the sacred history and make it their own as they bring the ongoing narrative of their actions into harmony with the conduct of biblical exemplars.

In preaching that they act as characters in the biblical stories did, Gregory discloses how his hearers can extend their participation in the festal events—and the encounters with God present within them—beyond liturgical observances and into their daily lives. In this way their everyday moral and spiritual practices become a continued participation in the biblical narrative and inscribe them into the story of salvation history. Once the connections are made in the context of liturgy, the faithful can through further mimetic activity continue to keep the feast and the communion with God it brings them. Thus, in Oration 40.43 Gregory identifies the newly baptized with people Jesus heals and raises from the dead and exhorts them to refrain from sin so as not to fall back into their previous illness or an even worse condition. Yesterday, he says, they were the same as the hemorrhaging woman, the paralytic and dead Lazarus. Today through baptism Christ has brought them to a new life in which they are called to persevere. Notice that in this text the exemplars to be imitated are not saints but sinners, broken people who started from the same unpromising point as average members of any congregation. People in Gregory's audience can imitate these exemplars by persevering in newfound wholeness through the avoidance of sin, that is by practicing daily acts and habits of virtue. The very brokenness they share with the hemorrhaging woman and the paralytic has become the starting point of a pattern of conduct that all can follow to attain salvation, sanctification, and communion with God. In such Christian mimesis, what matters is not whether the exemplars begin as saints or sinners but where their stories end.

However, imitation of saints and of Christ remain central for Gregory. It is essential to note that he and his contemporaries have in mind the imitation of *virtues*. They exhort the faithful to model their dispositions and behavior upon the saints' good character traits, just, devout and loving actions, and habits of morally excellent conduct. For the Cappadocians, imitation of the saints is ultimately imitation of Christ, and this mimesis is a matter of practicing virtues since Christ contains perfectly in himself the whole "circle of the virtues" (Oration 45.13), which in him are harmoniously commingled with each other. To act virtuously is to receive the grace of Christ and participate in his life.

Virtues also delineate the diversity in unity of human holiness. There are many virtuous character traits and patterns of activity, each of which can become a way to salvation. In several places Gregory provides lists of virtues or exemplary persons and actions and invites his hearers to choose the ones that fit their own character and circumstances. These lists map the diverse paths that lead to the eternal kingdom and show how the spiritual journey brings very different people together by leading them to the same goal in Christ. Such texts reveal the pastoral sensitivity Gregory discusses at length in Oration 2, *In Defense of his Flight*, which is the earliest Christian treatise on the priesthood. There Gregory analyzes the complex diversity of his congregation and shows awareness of the spiritual needs of different kinds of people. He says that a pastor needs great discernment, like a physician able to prescribe the right remedy for each patient, mindful that the same drug could heal one person but kill another.

In the *Festal Orations* the people who took part in the events celebrated, such as the shepherds and magi, become the exemplary figures. Gregory challenges his congregation to imitate their devotion during the liturgical celebration and afterwards to follow other patterns in their conduct so as to keep the "feast after the feast." In Oration 45.23 he exhorts his listeners to offer themselves to God, which involves a willingness to bear the cross, to suffer and die for Christ's sake. Then in paragraphs 24–25 he proposes as models a long list of characters in the stories of the Lord's passion, death, burial, resurrection and ascension. These two paragraphs follow the sequence of the paschal story and make several interesting points along the way. Echoing the theme in §23, §24 begins, "If you are Simon of Cyrene, take up the cross and follow." Gregory includes a number of figures who exemplify devotion and worship, such as Joseph of Arimathea who buries Christ's body, Peter and John who race each other to the tomb, and the angels who marvel at the ascension of God incarnate. Yet he recognizes that some in his congregation may be like the thief who though sinful shares Christ's sufferings and thus "steals" salvation, or like Thomas who becomes separated from the other disciples and doubts the resurrection but later sees and believes. Along with the devout, the preacher includes those struggling with grave sin or wrestling with doubt in the process of festal celebration and saving transformation. The long list in his sermon serves to unite his congregation, drawing them together toward shared life in God's future kingdom.

The intensity and directness with which Gregory identifies members of his audience with biblical exemplars is striking and significant. Marc van Uytfanghe identifies three kinds of typological language that connect more recent saints with biblical heroes in Merovingian hagiographies. The first and boldest kind is the direct transposition of the biblical figure's name to a saint, often with qualifying words like "new" or "another," as when Paul calls Christ the "new Adam" [1 Cor 15.45]. Merovingian hagiographers use this kind of language very sparingly; they dare not place their local saints on the same level as the renowned biblical exemplars. Instead they prefer the second and third kinds of typology, in which saints are said to be *like* biblical figures, or certain of their actions are compared to actions in Scripture that have similar patterns.[28] In contrast, Gregory characteristically transfers the names of biblical figures directly to his contemporaries. In Oration 40.33, cited above, he names the newly baptized in his audience as those Jesus has healed and raised to life.

> Yesterday you were dried up by the vigor of a hemorrhage, ... Today ... you are stanched, for you touched Christ's hem and the flow stopped. ...

> Yesterday you were thrown onto a bed ... and you had no human being to throw you into the pool. ... Today you have found a human being, the same one who is also God. ...

> "Lazarus, come out." Lying in a tomb, you have heard the great voice ... and you have come forth. ...

In Oration 45.24–25 the identification of Gregory's hearers with characters in the passion story is just as immediate: "If you are Simon of Cyrene, ... if you are crucified with him as a thief, ... if you are Joseph from Arimathea," and so on. Such texts reveal the extent to which Gregory saw his community as participating in the biblical world and its stories.

A Feast without the Liturgical Calendar?

Gregory sees himself and his fellow Christians as living in a world full of large and small opportunities to enter into the saving narra-

[28]Marc van Uytfanghe, *Stylisation biblique et condition humaine dans l'hagiographie mérovingienne [600–750]* (Brussels: WLSK, 1987), 18.

tive of biblical history through mimesis. In Oration 19, a sermon occasioned by the presence of the tax assessor Julian in Nazianzus and the political negotiations required to preserve tax exemption for clergy and monastics, Gregory shows that festal mimesis can occur even without a feast day. It becomes possible when circumstances in ordinary secular life imitate the patterns of festal events and thereby allow people to follow the paths of biblical story to a saving participation in a major salvation-historical event. Gregory unites the assessor's visit to his hometown with the imperial census for purposes of tax assessment that occasioned Christ's birth in Bethlehem. He declares that Julian's visit to the townspeople brings with it the presence of Christ's birth and all its saving grace.

> Now angels rejoice, now shepherds are dazzled by the radiance, now a star from the east races to the greatest and unapproachable light, now magi fall down and present gifts and recognize the king of all and adjudge him king of heaven thanks to the glorious testimony of the star. . . . Come then, let us join them in adoration. . . . Now Christ is born to you and is God and becomes human and sojourns among humankind.[29]

Throughout the sermon, Gregory exhorts the different kinds of people who are present, rich and poor, assessor and taxpayers, leaders and followers, to fulfill their duties justly and with reverence toward God. He tells them that by expressing their Christian priorities in the performance of mundane financial and political tasks they can enter into the joy and grace of Christmas.

For Gregory ubiquitous mimetic opportunities such as this are grounded in the incarnation itself. In Christ, God becomes present in the most ordinary of human activities. Oration 37.2 says that when Jesus is tired he blesses fatigue, when he sleeps he blesses sleep

---

[29]Oration 19.12–13, trans. Vinson, 105, modified.

too, and when he weeps he blesses tears.[30] Christians receive these blessings through mimesis, by choosing to perform their everyday actions as activities shared with their Savior. Actions approached and experienced in this way will be done differently, bringing personal sanctification and just and loving treatment of neighbors.

In the early church each virtue had its biblical exemplars. Certain biblical characters became standard representatives of different virtues, for instance faithful Abraham, hospitable Rahab, meek Moses and zealous Phineas. In Oration 14.2–4 Gregory includes these and many others, along with Christ the all-encompassing exemplar, in a long list that maps many different mimetic paths to salvation. He connects each virtue with its biblical model and notes that each leads to one of the eschatological "dwelling places with the Father" of John 14.2.

> Each of these virtues is one path to salvation, and leads, surely, towards one of the blessed, eternal dwellings; just as there are different chosen forms of life, so there are many "dwelling places" with God, distributed and allotted to each person according to his merit. So let one person cultivate this virtue, the other that, another several, still another all of them—if that is possible! Let each one simply walk on the way, and reach out for what is ahead, and let him follow the footsteps of the one who leads the way so clearly, who makes it straight and guides us by the narrow path and gate to the broad plain of blessedness in the world to come.[31]

The diverse people brought together in Gregory's congregations thus foreshadow the unity in diversity of the community eternally blessed in the eschaton. For him festal mimesis forms part of a much larger pattern that encompasses the biblical characters and narratives and ordinary Christian people and their life stories within the

---

[30]*Patrologia graeca* 36:284C. *Patrologia graeca* will hereafter be referred to as PG.
[31]Trans. Daley, 78.

overarching narrative of salvation history itself. All these persons, events and stories are at least potentially united to each other in Christ through links of typology and mimetic activity. Many and varied paths can lead people of all kinds from very different starting places to a shared life in the kingdom of God.

Rhetoric and Theology

Let us now turn from Gregory's work as festal celebrant to examine the theological reflection in his festal homilies. Gregory makes creative use of his considerable literary, philosophical and rhetorical talent and training as he makes various attempts to express what he can of the mysteries of the Trinity, Jesus Christ, and the human person. Though always mindful that the divine mystery is largely incomprehensible and ineffable, he is aware of his gift for λόγοι (words and discourse), as we have seen. His theological writings are didactic and sometimes polemical, but they are above all doxological. He uses logical argumentation to articulate theology but also prayer and praise, poetry and rhetorical prose. Immersed as he is in the literary forms of the Second Sophistic, the fashionable rhetorical technique of his time, in many texts he employs the balanced clauses and antithetical structures of rhetorical Greek to speak of the Trinity and other topics. During his long education in Athens he absorbed these structures into his mind so thoroughly that they molded his way of thinking. He was thus able to transform them from literary ornament to theological method.

Balance and symmetry were prized in many aspects of Greek culture, including everything from art to law, ethics to medicine.[32] The

[32]G.R. Lloyd, *Polarity and Analogy: Two Types of Argumentation in Greek Thought* (Cambridge: Cambridge University Press, 1966), 15–171; and Richard Garner, *Law and Society in Classical Athens* (New York: St Martin's, 1987), 75–83. On 75, Garner observes that "the Greeks imposed many different sorts of binary divisions on the world. Some were contrasting, carefully matched and balanced. Some . . . examples may seem somehow unnatural or merely forced, but this is precisely what makes the phenomenon so important."

men/de construction that plays a large role in Greek language and literature, especially in Late Antique rhetorical Greek, expresses this sense of balance.[33] Gregory transforms a common figure of speech, antithesis, into a new "logic" or "grammar" for speaking about the Trinity and other theological topics. He often uses it to juxtapose and balance two different truth claims so as to affirm both together in such a way that they reinforce each other instead of conflicting. Thus, he does not start from the unity of essence in God and argue to the threeness of persons, nor does he start from the three persons and argue to the one essence. Instead he begins by declaring that the divinity is simultaneously one in three and three in one. Vladimir Lossky, who quotes him extensively, is right to emphasize antimony as a structural element in Gregory's Trinitarian theology.[34]

However, Lossky is mistaken in identifying antinomy as exclusively apophatic.[35] Some of Gregory's antinomies are in fact neither/nor statements, rejecting the opposite errors of Sabellianism and Arianism, or "Jewish" unitarianism and "pagan" polytheism within Christian theology. Yet such double negations establish the context for affirming the mean between the extremes. For example, in Oration 39.8 he says:

> When I say "God," I mean Father and Son and Holy Spirit. The divinity is not diffused beyond these, lest we introduce a crowd of gods, but nor is it limited to fewer than these, lest we be condemned to a poverty of divinity, either Judaizing because of the monarchy or hellenizing because of the abundance. For the evil is alike in both cases, though it is found in opposites.

---

[33]Classical and patristic Greek use *men* and *de* to juxtapose clauses or sentences and balance them against each other. A possible translation is, "on the one hand/on the other hand."

[34]Vladimir Lossky, *The Mystical Theology of the Eastern Church* (Cambridge: James Clark and Co., 1957), 44–66.

[35]Lossky, *Mystical Theology*, 42–43.

Similarly, in Oration 39.11 he says, "Let both the contraction of Sabellius and the division of Arius be equally far from us, the evils that are diametrically opposed yet equal in impiety."[36] However, more often his antinomies are double affirmations, both/and statements intended to combine theological affirmations while recognizing the mystery between them that holds them together. For instance, he affirms that God is both one and three, and that Christ is fully divine and fully human. His antinomic theology is an eloquent and flexible method for expressing the emphatic doctrinal affirmations that Gregory loves to make while acknowledging the apophatic context that surrounds them.

The Trinity

Many things could be said regarding Gregory's immensely creative, multifaceted and foundational thought about how God is Trinity.[37] We will focus on three topics that are distinctive of him and of interest to contemporary theologians: (1) God as both one and three; (2) divine activity, by which God is known and encountered in the created world, as both one and three; and (3) human community as an image of the Holy Trinity. We will begin by discussing (1) and (2) together.

In one of his earlier discourses he speaks of divine attributes as both singular and plural, describing the Trinity as follows:

Lives and life, lights and light, goods and good, glories and glory; true and truth and Spirit of truth, holy ones and holiness itself; each one is God if contemplated alone, with the

---

[36]See also Oration 2.36–37, 40.42, and 42.16.

[37]See Daley, *Gregory of Nazianzus,* 41–50, and Christopher Beeley, *Gregory of Nazianzus on the Trinity and the Knowledge of God* (Oxford: Oxford University Press, 2008), chap. 4. Let me thank Christopher Beeley for sharing his work with me in manuscript.

intellect dividing undivided entities; the three [are contemplated] as one God through their identity of movement and of nature when apprehended with each other (Oration 23.11).[38]

This text shows how Gregory's understanding of the Trinity differs from that of the later, exclusively Western "Athanasian" Creed, which objects to naming divine attributes in the plural.[39] Yet notice how Gregory's plurals are all combined with singulars. As Gregory names the divine characteristics of three distinct persons, he takes care to affirm their oneness. He notes that in contemplation, that is in prayer or theological reflection, which for him are surely interconnected, one can perceive each of the persons as God but also all three together as one God. Though the human mind can think of the persons as separate, in reality, he declares, they are inseparable in nature and movement, by which he surely means being and activity. Yet this does not mean the hypostases are indistinguishable. When Gregory names "true and truth and Spirit of truth," he refers to them in the standard sequential order the Cappadocians identify in divine activity *ad extra*: from the Father, through the Son, in the Holy Spirit. This pattern of self-manifestation follows the same sequence as the relations of origin by which the divine persons are distinguished and related to each other. So they are not indistinguishable or interchangeable in their common activity, which itself has a threefold structure that reveals them as distinct persons in the created world.

In the Oration 39, his discussion of the Trinity begins with a simultaneous affirmation of oneness and threeness.

When I speak of God, be struck from all sides by the lightning flash (περιαστράφθητε) of one light and also three; three in regard to the individualities (ἰδιότητας), that is

---

[38]Sources chrétiennes 270:302. Sources chrétiennes will hereafter be referred to as SC.

[39]Jaroslav Pelikan and Valerie Hotchkiss, eds., *Creeds and Confessions of Faith in the Christian Tradition* (New Haven: Yale University Press, 2003), 1:675–77.

hypostases, if one prefers to call them this, or persons, for we will not struggle with our comrades about the names as long as the syllables convey the same idea; but one if one speaks of the essence, that is the divinity. For they are divided undividedly, if I may speak thus, and united in division. For the divinity is one in three, and the three are one, in whom the divinity is, or, to speak more precisely, who are the divinity. But we omit the excesses and omissions, neither making the union a fusion, nor the division a separation. Let both the contraction of Sabellius and the division of Arius be equally far from us, the evils that are diametrically opposed yet equal in impiety. For why is it necessary to either fuse God together wrongly or cut him up into inequalities? (Oration 39.11).

In this passage Gregory carries further the points he made in Oration 23.11. He specifies that the threeness pertains to the hypostases and the oneness to the essence. He identifies what he regards as correct Trinitarian terminology while noting that consensus about concepts is more important than use of the same vocabulary. At the end he clarifies his position further by locating it as the mean between two opposing errors.

The intensity and immediacy of the image he uses to introduce this discussion are particularly significant. He invites his listeners to "be struck from all sides by the lightning flash" (περιαστράφθητε) of the one divine light yet also by three divine lights. This powerful image suggests that the divine persons surround Gregory's congregation as three overwhelming lights that are also one light enveloping them. Such language brings us very far from imagining a single indistinguishable activity coming down from a Trinity isolated within itself from the created world. Gregory is saying that the three divine persons who are one God are present in the liturgical celebration of a great feast as intensely as sheets of lightning striking the ground all around the center of an extreme thunderstorm in the midwestern United States, and that he and his listeners stand at that storm's center. Browne and Swallow's translation of this phrase as "be illumined at once by one flash of light and by three"[40] does not convey this adequately. Gregory uses words carefully and does not attach prepositions to verbs without meaning as some Late Antique writers may do. The περὶ is important in this text, and we will see it again in another important Trinitarian passage in the sermon he preached the next day, Oration 40. Both of these texts may be alluding to Luke 2.9, which he quotes in Oration 39.14: "Therefore at his birth we kept festival, both I the leader of the feast, and you, and all that is in the world and above the world. With the star we ran, and with the magi we worshipped [Matt 2.8–11], and with the shepherds we were surrounded by light (περιελάμφθημεν), and with the angels we gave glory [Luke 2.9–14]."

Near the end of Oration 40, a long and eloquent exhortation to be baptized that Gregory preached in the Church of the Holy Apostles, newly restored to the Nicene faith, he makes a solemn confession of the Trinitarian faith he will entrust to those he baptizes. The context of festal celebration and union with Christ through baptism provides an appropriate setting for Gregory's extraordinary depiction of how he contemplates God as three and as one. Here he revisits the simultaneous affirmation of divine unity and plurality we read in Oration 23.11 but with greater clarity, detail and intensity.

> This I give you as a companion and protector for all your life, the one divinity and power, found in unity in the three, and gathering together the three as distinct; neither uneven in essences or natures, nor increased or decreased by superiorities or inferiorities; from every perspective equal, from every perspective the same, as the beauty and greatness of heaven is one; an infinite coalescence of three infinites; each God when considered in himself; as the Father so the Son, as the Son so the Holy Spirit; each preserving his properties.

[40]C.G. Browne and J.E. Swallow, trans., *St Gregory of Nazianzen, Nicene and Post-Nicene Fathers,* Series 2 (Grand Rapids, MI: Eerdmans, 1983), 7:355. Hereafter *NPNF*[2].

The three are God when known together, each God because of the consubstantiality, one God because of the monarchy. When I first know the one I am also illumined from all sides (περιλάμπομαι) by the three; when I first distinguish the three I am also carried back to the one. When I picture one of the three I consider this the whole, and my eyes are filled, and the greater part has escaped me. I cannot grasp the greatness of that one so as to grant something greater to the rest. When I bring the three together in contemplation, I see one torch and am unable to divide or measure the united light (Oration 40.41).

Gregory speaks of how his spiritual gaze moves back and forth between God as one and the three persons, and between each divine person and all of them together, though he knows that most of what he contemplates escapes his grasp. He invites those he will lead into full communion with the church to follow him into an immensely rich Trinitarian spirituality in which each hypostasis can be known directly and appears as the whole of God, yet the three are also manifest as related to each other in a sequential order, and as being one God. Again Gregory uses a peri-compound to speak of the hypostases as three lights surrounding him, adding that together they constitute one undivided light. And again Browne and Swallow, who render περιλάμπομαι simply as "I am illumined,"[41] miss the immediate and all-encompassing character of the triune presence by missing the preposition. This is the same verb used in Luke 2.9 to speak of the glory of the Lord shining all around the shepherds. Since God is infinite, this light, and by implication any one of the divine hypostases or the one divine nature as such, cannot be measured quantitatively or divided into circumscribed parts. The language of contemplation and light shows further that this text refers not only to the Trinity in itself but also to its self-manifestation and activity

[41]Browne and Swallow, *NPNF²* 7:375.

in the world in a way capable of being perceived by created beings like Gregory and his congregation.

The texts we have studied from Orations 23, 39 and 40 can help us understand a similar passage in Oration 31, the *Fifth Theological Oration*, which boldly confesses the full divinity of the Holy Spirit and Gregory's doctrine of the Trinity. In §3 he summarizes his Trinitarian position in a way that adds precision and clarity to what he said earlier in Oration 23.11.

> He "was the true light that illumines every human being coming into the world" [John 1.9]—the Father. He "was the true light that illumines every human being coming into the world"—the Son. He "was the true light that illumines every human being coming into the world"—the other Advocate [John 14.16, 26]. Was and was and was, but was one. Light and light and light, but one light and one God. This is indeed what David perceived long ago when he said, "In your light we see light" [Ps 35.10]. As for us, now we also have seen and we proclaim, from the light of the Father grasping the light of the Son in the light of the Spirit, a concise and simple theology of the Trinity.[42]

Again Gregory speaks of the persons as three lights yet one God. When he says "but one light," this statement is juxtaposed antithetically to the statements about threeness that precede it and must not be understood as negating or superseding them. The interpretation of Psalm 35.10 that follows makes this clear. Gregory proclaims that he receives light from the divine persons in the usual sequential order. From the Father's light he grasps the Son's light in the Spirit's light. This brings him into direct and distinct encounters with all three persons in a single act of contemplation. Though he looks most immediately toward the Son, who is the Father's Logos and revealer,

[42]SC 250:280.

he is illumined from all sides by the three. He finds himself in the center of their common self-revelatory activity, in which each of them participates in a unique way.

These texts show that Gregory perceives the Trinity in at least two different ways, both of which reveal God's activity that comes down to the created world where he can see it. First, he sees both one light and three. That means that each of the divine persons is present to him and acts directly and immediately. The action of each is distinct, though they all act jointly, "as if among three suns conjoined to each other there were one commingling of light" (Oration 31.14). Secondly, there is one divine activity to which each person contributes in a distinct way, that proceeds from the Father, through the Son, in the Holy Spirit. In Oration 23.11 and 31.3, 14 Gregory places each of these patterns side by side. In Oration 40.41 he alludes to a variety of ways in which the Trinity is manifest to him. Clearly, God is free to act in this world and to reveal himself to his saints in a variety of ways.

Gregory also speaks of the divine persons sharing distinctively in common activities as recounted in Scripture. Father and Son collaborate with each other, and so do Son and Spirit:

For indeed Scripture says that he was given up [Rom 4.25, 1 Cor 11.3], but it is also written that he gave himself up [Gal 2.20, Eph 5.2, 25]; and he was raised and taken up to heaven by the Father [Acts 17.31, Rom 4.24, Mark 16.19], but he also resurrected himself and ascended there again [Matt 22.6, Mark 16, 9, 19]. For one is the Father's good will, the other is his own power (Oration 45.27).

Christ is born, the Spirit is his forerunner [Luke 1.31]; Christ is baptized, the Spirit bears him witness [Matt 3.13–17, Luke 3.21–22]; Christ is tempted, the Spirit leads him up [Matt 4.1, Luke 4.2]; Christ performs miracles, the Spirit accompanies him [Matt 12.22, 28]; Christ ascends, the Spirit fills his place [Acts 1.9, 2.3–4] (Oration 31.29).[43]

Let us now turn to (3) the Trinity and human community. Texts cited above have shown how Gregory encounters the Trinity as one and three together, and thinks of the divine persons' actions as both distinctive and united. This model portrays the Trinity in a way that can serve as a model for community among human beings. Gregory developed this idea early in his ministry when assisting his father at Nazianzus. He preached a sermon entitled the *First Oration on Peace*, intended to heal a schism between Gregory the Elder and some local monks over Trinitarian doctrine. The younger Gregory, who had close ties with those on both sides, mediated a reconciliation in which both made concessions. His oration celebrates, strengthens and ratifies the agreement and in this context offers profound theological reflection on the value and meaning of peace and harmony in the human community. He praises the renewed concord of the congregation as linking them to God who is one and three: "Now, belonging to the One we have become one, and belonging to the Trinity we have come to be the same in nature and in soul and in honor"[44] (Oration 6.4). This Trinitarian language follows the pattern noted in texts cited above, an antinomical juxtaposition of the unity and Trinity of God so as to affirm both equally. The connection of these divine characteristics with the unity and communal harmony of the congregation suggests that a human community with this character imitates and thus belongs to, or indeed participates in, the unity in diversity of the Godhead.

Later in the same homily, Gregory makes this more explicit as he exhorts his audience to strengthen and preserve their newfound peace. He encourages them to follow the examples of God, and of

[43]Frederick Williams and Lionel Wickham, trans., *St Gregory of Nazianzus: The Five Theological Orations and Two Letters to Cledonius* (Crestwood, NY: SVS Press, 2002), 139.
[44]SC 405:130.

angels who are illumined by God and thus like God live in unity, without division or conflict among themselves. He warns them to avoid the example and influence of the fallen angels, who broke their peace with God and who instigate conflicts among human beings. Gregory then returns to the example of the holy angels and shows how this harmonious community participates in the life of the Trinity, as do human communities that love peace and reject conflict.

"The angels who do not fall," he says,

> remain in their own condition, which first is peace and absence of division, having received unity as a gift of the Holy Trinity, from which also comes their illumination. For it is one God and is believed to be such, no less because of its harmony (ὁμόνοιαν) than because of its sameness of essence. So those [people] belong to God and are close to divine realities who are shown as embracing the good of peace and rejecting the opposite, division[45] (Oration 6.13).

The harmony named here characterizes the Trinity as community while the sameness of essence characterizes God as one. Gregory goes on to identify peace in human community as the image and likeness of God, thereby providing an early, ground-breaking example of a favorite theme among contemporary theologians, humankind as image of the Trinity.

> Only one thing can constrain us to such benevolence and harmony (συμφωνίας), the imitation of God and of divine realities. Toward this alone it is prudent for the soul to look, having come into being according to the image of God, that it may preserve its nobility as far as possible through inclination toward the divine and, to the extent it is able, likeness to it[46] (Oration 6.13).

[45]SC 405:154–56.
[46]SC 405:156.

The divine perfection that people are invited to share here is harmony, whose model in God can only be the communal life of the Trinity. Here Gregory makes a small beginning to Trinitarian anthropology. He will work out the foundations for this conclusion later in Constantinople, in the *Festal Orations* and the *Theological Orations*.

A Systematic Theology in a Nutshell

Gregory summarizes his understanding of creation and redemption in Oration 38.7–13 and repeats the same material verbatim in Oration 45.3–9. In characteristically lapidary phrases, he briefly describes the transcendent God, creation of the angelic and material worlds, the human created as microcosm, the fall, salvation history, the incarnation, and salvation in Christ. Let us review these themes, in some cases placing them in the larger context of Gregory's writings.

He begins in Oration 38.7–8 by speaking of God in himself, in contrast to the created world. God transcends the time that structures the created universe, and God alone is truly "being." It follows that we must approach the divine by the apophatic way, a point Gregory makes here, as in the *First Theological Oration*, before he begins theologizing. These paragraphs manifest Gregory's debt to Plato. Through purification and desire—more Platonic themes—we can draw near to the divine so that indeed "God [is] united with gods." Unlike Gregory of Nyssa, who usually avoids deification language, Gregory Nazianzen glories in it. And here again he speaks of God appearing like lightning, a brilliant light surrounding the beholder that is grasped only for a moment, "a swift bolt of lightning that does not remain."

Gregory cannot remain in such rarified heights for long. So he declares that "this is enough philosophizing about God at present," and that he will turn from "theology" to "economy." Significantly, for him the term "economy," which names how God is active in the created world and in history, refers first to the doctrine of the Trinity: "When I say 'God,' I mean Father and Son and Holy Spirit" (Oration 38.8). This statement underlines the point discussed above, that for Gregory God is manifest and active in the creation precisely as Trinity.

Theological Anthropology

Gregory continues in a Platonic vein in Oration 38.9–10 when he speaks of God's creation; he says that the divine Good naturally seeks to spread its goodness, and he divides the creation into intelligible and sense-perceptible worlds. The angelic world is created first, and then the visible, material world. Both are good and harmonious, yet the angels are naturally close to God, while the earth is, in contrast, far from him. Yet in §11, Gregory asserts that the human being, who participates in both, was created to unite the intelligible and sense-perceptible worlds. The human is thus "a kind of second world," that is a microcosm, sharing in every level of created reality, and therefore is enabled to serve as the connecting link, to unite all created things and offer them to God.

Here as elsewhere, Gregory expresses ambivalence about the human body. The human person, he says, is "spirit on account of grace"; yet is also given flesh to curb his pride, since flesh makes him suffer. This attitude is best understood in light of a passage from Oration 14, where he has described lepers, people disfigured, tormented and ostracized because of physical disease and disability. In this context he reflects on his experience of embodied existence.

> How I am connected to this body, I do not know, nor do I understand how I can be an image of God, and still be mingled with this filthy clay; when it is in good condition, it wars against me, and when it is itself under attack, it causes me grief! I love it as my fellow servant, but struggle against it

as an enemy; I flee it as something enslaved, just as I am, but I show it reverence as called, with me, to the same inheritance. I long that it be dissolved, and yet I have no other helper to use in striving for what is best, since I know what I was made for, and know that I must ascend towards God through my actions.[47]

That is, Gregory's body is precisely the means through which he acts in the world to practice virtue and to be of service. Moreover, Gregory affirms that lepers are members of Christ. Bodily service given to them is in fact given to Christ (Oration 14.40, citing Matt 25.35–36), which presupposes that Christ dwells in their bodies and makes them his own. Oration 38.11 ends by confessing the resurrection of the body, the greatest possible affirmation of its value.

Oration 38.12 is a fascinating commentary on Genesis 2–3. Gregory begins by affirming that God gives humans freedom so that they would share with him the credit for being sources of good. In Platonic fashion, he interprets tending the garden to mean cultivation of divine thoughts. Then, interestingly, he suggests, like Irenaeus,[48] that Adam and Eve were children in Paradise:

God gave him a law as material on which his self-determination could work, and the law was a commandment indicating which plants he could possess and which one he was not to touch. And that was the tree of knowledge [Gen 2.16–17], which was neither planted from the beginning in an evil way nor forbidden through envy ... but would be good if possessed at the right time. For the tree is contemplation, according to my own contemplation, which is only safe for those of mature disposition to undertake; but it is not good for those who are still simpler and those greedy in their

[47]Oration 14.6; trans. Daley, 79; PG 35:865A–B.
[48]*Against Heresies* 4.38–39; Adelin Rousseau, ed., *Irénée de Lyon: Contre les hérésies, livre IV* (SC 100; Paris: Editions du Cerf, 1965), 2:942–973.

desire, just as adult food is not useful for those who are still tender and in need of milk.

God's plan was to educate their freedom by letting them practice not eating from the tree of knowledge. In this way, they would have grown to adulthood and been prepared to eat from it, just as an ascetic grows through practice of the virtues and resistance to temptations, so as to be ready for the contemplation for which humankind was indeed created. Adam and Eve's sin was grasping at contemplation too soon, like a young, overly zealous monk who, like them, is headed for a fall.

Note that Gregory does not lay exclusive blame for the fall on Eve. He blames "the devil's envy," adding compassionately that the first woman suffered "spiteful treatment" as well as inflicting it on Adam. Instead of passing the blame to another as Adam did (Gen 3.12), like a good desert father Gregory blames himself. He identifies himself with fallen Adam, exclaiming, "Alas for my weakness, for that of the first father is mine!"

Oration 38.12 also contains the word παχύτης, a key term in Gregory's anthropology and Christology that resists easy translation. Gregory says that the "tunics of skin" in which God clothed fallen Adam and Eve are "perhaps the more coarse (παχυτέραν) and mortal and rebellious flesh." In other words, the body itself underwent a transformation as a result of sin. It became subject to death and came to resist God, the soul and its own spiritualization. The word παχύτης points to these characteristics of fallen flesh. I have usually followed Brian Daley's example and translated it "coarseness." It can mean heaviness, denseness, grossness, or coarseness, in contrast to the character of redeemed flesh that is united to soul in glorifying God: lightness and refinement. Gregory of Nyssa neatly summarizes the contrast in *The Life of Moses*:

Bodies, once they have received the initial thrust downward, are driven downward by themselves with greater speed without any additional help as long as . . . no resistance to their downward thrust is encountered. Similarly, the soul moves in the opposite direction. Once it is released from its earthly attachment, it becomes light and swift for its movement upward, soaring from below up to the heights.[49]

Gregory of Nyssa adds in the next paragraph that once the downward pull is overcome through ascetic effort, desire for God naturally draws the whole human person ever upward into eternal growth in God. The downward pull he describes pertains specifically to our fallen condition, and Gregory of Nazianzus refers to it as παχύτης, heaviness.

Note that the problem is with fallen flesh, not embodiment as such; for both Gregorys the body can indeed be redeemed, returned to its pre-lapsarian condition. Other occurrences of forms of παχύτης in this book show how this redemption happens. Within the person of Christ the human rational soul serves as a mediator, uniting the divinity to the coarseness of the flesh (Oration 39.12). After his resurrection, Christ's body becomes deiform and is "without fleshly coarseness" (Oration 41.45). Gregory of Nazianzus hopes that we will in the end share Christ's risen mode of existence, but in the meantime our fallen flesh's coarseness holds our mind captive, so that we cannot contemplate God without God's help (Oration 45.11). Finally, he declares that when people are completely unspiritual, the coarseness has spread from their flesh to their minds (Oration 45.12). So, ultimately, the problem is misuse of free choice, not embodiment.

---

[49]Herbert Musurillo, ed., *Gregorii Nysseni Opera VII.I: De Vita Moysis* (Leiden: Brill, 1964), 112; Gregory of Nyssa, *The Life of Moses* (trans. A.J. Malherbe and E. Ferguson; San Francisco: Harper, 2006), 102. Their translation simplifies grammatical complications in the Greek to make the meaning clear in English.

The Person and Work of Christ

Oration 38.13 begins with a summary of salvation history, noting that nothing God did as recounted in the Hebrew Bible was enough to overcome the enormities of human sin. So God provided a greater help in Christ's incarnation. "An innovation is made to natures," Gregory says in Oration 39.13, "and God became human ... ; not changing what he was, for he is immutable, but assuming what he was not, for he loves humankind." That is, he remains God but takes upon himself humanity. This divine descent to our level turns the cosmic hierarchy upside down; it is a new work of God, greater than creation itself. Thus, "he shares with us a second communion, much more paradoxical than the first; then he gave us a share in what is superior, now he shares in what is inferior. This is more godlike than the first; this, to those who can understand, is more exalted" (Oration 38.13).

"O the new mixture (μίξεως)! O the paradoxical blending (κράσεως)!" Gregory exclaims, "He who is comes into being, and the uncreated is created, and the uncontained is contained, through the intervention of the rational soul, which mediates between the divinity and the coarseness (παχύτητι) of flesh" (Oration 38.13). The words translated here as "mixture" and "blending" are Stoic technical terms. They refer to a kind of mixing in which two ingredients are combined so that they permeate each other, yet each retains its own nature and characteristics, so they could be separated while retaining their integrity. For example, dried beans and peas can be stirred together while remaining beans and peas. Gregory uses this language to indicate how the divine and human natures in Christ are completely united, yet each preserves its own character. The Stoic terminology was later understood differently by the Council of Chalcedon (451), which ruled out its further use in Christology. It was subsequently replaced by the term *perichoresis*, which means essentially the same as what Gregory meant by "mixture" and "blending."[50]

[50]See N.V. Harrison, "*Perichoresis* in the Greek Fathers," *St Vladimir's Theological*

The text quoted above also speaks of Christ's human rational soul as mediating between the divinity and the flesh, since it has enough in common with both to bring them together. In a number of places, Gregory ascribes the function of uniting the two to the human soul, an unusual idea characteristic of his Christology. For instance, in Oration 29.19, he says, "Through the medium of the mind he had dealings with the flesh, being made that God on earth, which is Man."[51] Perhaps he borrows this idea from Origen, an influence other fathers sought to avoid.[52]

Gregory of Nazianzus is exceptionally clear and insightful in describing how it is that Christ saves us. His classic formula appears in Letter 101, where he says, "What is not assumed is not healed, but what is united to God, that is also saved."[53] In other words, Christ saves every part of the human person by uniting it with his divinity. So if he lacked part of our humanity, such as a human mind, he would not be able to save. As Gregory says in Oration 40.45, "He is a whole human being, and the same [person] is also God, on behalf of the whole sufferer, that salvation may be granted to the whole of you." His humanity is the same as ours and is united to ours, which brings us into contact with God. Then the same divine life present in us works in two opposite ways; it purifies out what is bad in us and sanctifies what is good: "He bears the whole of me, along with all that is mine, in himself, so that he may consume within himself the meaner element, as fire consumes wax or the sun the ground mist, and so that I may share in what is his through the intermingling" (Oration 30.6).[54]

By sharing in our condition and enabling us to share in his, Christ accomplishes an exchange between the head and the body,

Quarterly 35 (1991): 53–65.

[51]Trans. Williams and Wickham, 86; SC 250:218.

[52]*On First Principles* 2.6.3–4; Herwig Görgemanns and Heinrich Karpp, eds., *Origenes Vier Bücher von den Prinzipien* (Darmstadt: Wissenschaftliche Buchgesellschaft, 1976), 360–366.

[53]Letter 101, in Paul Gallay, ed., *Grégoire de Nazianze: Lettres théologiques* (SC 208; Paris: Editions du Cerf, 1974), 50.

[54]Trans. Williams and Wickham, 97; SC 250:236.

between himself and humankind. He takes to himself our slavery, sinfulness and curse so as to bestow on us his dignity, holiness and blessing.[55] In this context of shared life, the concept of exchange makes sense. Notions of Christ being punished in our place, which many Christians find troubling today, have no place in Gregory's thought.

The exchange extends so far that Christ assumes our death to bestow on us his resurrection. He descends to the lowest point of human existence—torment, death, and the grave—in order to bring up with himself.

> He assumed what is worse that he might give what is better. He became poor that we through his poverty might become rich. He took the form of a slave, that we might regain freedom. He descended that we might be lifted up, he was tempted that we might be victorious, he was dishonored to glorify us, he died to save us, he ascended to draw to himself us who lay below in the Fall of sin (Oration 1.5).

This is the reason why Gregory believes Christ had to die, a view he expresses with characteristic eloquence: "We needed a God made flesh and made dead, that we might live" (Oration 45.28). Note that it is the presence of God, the source of life, within death that is lifegiving. Gregory adds in the next paragraph, "A few drops of blood recreate the whole world and become for all human beings like a curdling agent to milk, binding and drawing us together into one" (Oration 45.29). The blood recreates because it is God's blood. It transforms humakind from a shifting, spilling liquid like milk into a compact solid like cheese. Once introduced into humankind, including even human death, the divine presence of Christ spreads throughout the whole and unites it, to vary the culinary metaphor, like yeast permeating a lump of dough and making it rise.

[55]Oration 30.5–6, trans. Williams and Wickham, 96–98; SC 250:232–38.

We now come to Gregory's most famous text about atonement, Oration 45.22, in which he critiques the wrong kind of exchange, the idea that Christ was a ransom paid to the devil, or indeed to God the Father. I will not repeat the text here; it is rather long and appears near the end of this book. However, let me explain the positive interpretation of atonement that Gregory proposes obscurely near the end of the paragraph by way of discussing Moses. He uses this metaphor to express the same theory we have been discussing. Moses attached a bronze serpent to a pole to cure deadly snakebites during Israel's wanderings in the wilderness. Those who looked up at the bronze serpent were healed (Num 21.9). Early Christians believed that the bronze serpent was attached crosswise to the pole, making the shape of a cross. For them this story became a standard symbol of Christ's crucifixion. So when Gregory talks about it he is still speaking indirectly about the cross. He says that the bronze serpent is actually a contrast to the cross instead of a straightforward representation of it. The bronze serpent was dead and caused the biting snakes to die too, but because he is God Christ remains the giver of life even when he hangs on the cross and lies in the tomb. Christ's divine life and divine presence inside the experience of human death overcome the power of sin, suffering, evil and death from within, so they are no longer able to destroy us or separate us from God. Gregory mocks "Hades," which may mean either the grave, the realm of the dead, or hell. Christ enters this realm, makes a new path out of it into the resurrection, and brings those he saves with him into eternal life.

Regarding the outcome of God's saving work, Gregory expresses hope. At the end of his theology in a nutshell, in Oration 38.12, he notes that Adam, who represents the whole human race, "gained a certain advantage from this [divine judgment]; death is also the cutting off of sin, that evil might not be immortal, so the punishment becomes love for humankind. For thus, I am persuaded, God punishes." Gregory takes for granted our eternal life and notes that God uses death to slay sin, thus freeing us from evil. If evil is gone after death, where is the punishment? In Oration 40.36, Gregory lists the threats of fire he finds in Scripture, then makes the following observation: "For all these fires belong to the destroying power [of God], unless some prefer even here to understand this fire as showing more love to humankind, in a way worthy of the punisher." He is less speculative than his friend Gregory of Nyssa, who affirms universal salvation. Nazianzen stops short of this daring claim, but he hints at the possibility.[56]

The Translations

Oration 1 is translated from Jean Bernardi's *Grégoire de Nazianze: Discours 1–3* (Sources chrétiennes 247; Paris: Editions du Cerf, 1978), 72–82. Orations 38 through 41 are translated from Claudio Moreschini's *Grégoire de Nazianze: Discours 38–41* (Sources chrétiennes 358; Paris: Editions du Cerf, 1990). In the absence of a modern critical edition, for Oration 45 we have relied upon J.P. Migne's *Patrologia graeca* 36:625–664.

[56]For further discussion of this point, see Metropolitan Kallistos Ware, "Dare We Hope for the Salvation of All?" in *idem, The Inner Kingdom* (Crestwood, NY: SVS Press, 2000), 193–215.

On Pascha and on His Slowness

1   It is the day of resurrection and an auspicious beginning. Let us be made brilliant by the feast and embrace each other. Let us call brothers even those who hate us,[1] and much more those who have done or suffered anything out of love for us. Let us concede all things to the resurrection. Let us grant pardon to each other, I who have been tyrannized by the good tyranny—for I add this now—and you who have tyrannized me well, if you blamed me in anything for my slowness, since perhaps it is better and more honorable than the quickness of others. For it is good both to draw back from God a little, like great Moses of old[2] and Jeremiah later,[3] and to run readily toward the one who calls, like Aaron[4] and Isaiah,[5] provided both are done piously, the first because of one's own weakness and the second because of the power of the one who calls.

2   A mystery anointed me. I drew back a little from the mystery, long enough to examine myself. And I enter with a mystery, bringing this good day as an ally for my cowardice and weakness, that he who today is risen from the dead may also make me new by the Spirit, and clothing me with the new human being[6] may give to the new creation,[7] to those born according to God,[8] a good molder

[1] Isa 66.5.
[2] Exod 4.13.
[3] Jer 1.6.
[4] Exod 4.27.
[5] Isa 6.8.
[6] Eph 4.23–24.
[7] 2 Cor 5.17.
[8] John 1.13.

and teacher, one who willingly both dies with Christ and rises with him.[9]

3   Yesterday the lamb was slaughtered, and the doorposts were anointed, and the Egyptians lamented the firstborn, and the destroyer passed over us, and the seal was awesome and venerable, and we were walled in by the precious blood. Today we have totally escaped Egypt and Pharaoh the harsh despot and the burdensome overseers, and we have been freed from the clay and the brick-making. And nobody hinders us from celebrating a feast of exodus for the Lord our God and keeping feast "not with the old leaven of malice and wickedness but with the unleavened bread of sincerity and truth,"[10] bringing nothing of the Egyptian and godless dough.[11]

4   Yesterday I was crucified with Christ, today I am glorified with him; yesterday I died with him, today I am made alive with him; yesterday I was buried with him, today I rise with him. But let us make an offering to the one who died and rose again for us. Perhaps you think I am speaking of gold or silver or tapestries or transparent precious stones, earthly matter that is in flux and remains below, of which the greater part always belongs to evil people and slaves of things below and of the ruler of this world.[12] Let us offer our own selves, the possession most precious to God and closest to him. Let us give back to the Image that which is according to the image,[13] recognizing our value, honoring the Archetype, knowing the power of the mystery and for whom Christ died.

[9]Rom 6.8.
[10]1 Cor 5.8.
[11]Exod 12.34.
[12]John 14.30.
[13]Gregory and many of the Greek fathers hold that the eternal Son, who became incarnate as Jesus Christ, is the Image of God in the strict sense, since he is of one essence with the Father and entirely like him. The divine Logos is thus the model according to which human beings have been created, so they are said to be made "according to the image."

5   Let us become like Christ, since Christ also became like us; let us become gods because of him, since he also because of us became human. He assumed what is worse that he might give what is better. He became poor that we through his poverty might become rich.[14] He took the form of a slave,[15] that we might regain freedom.[16] He descended that we might be lifted up, he was tempted that we might be victorious, he was dishonored to glorify us, he died to save us, he ascended to draw to himself us who lay below in the Fall of sin. Let us give everything, offer everything, to the one who gave himself as a ransom and an exchange for us.[17] But one can give nothing comparable to oneself, understanding the mystery and becoming because of him everything that he became because of us.

6   He offers you, as you see, a shepherd, for this is what the good shepherd[18] who lays down his life for his sheep[19] hopes and prays and asks for you who are under his authority. And he gives you himself double instead of single and makes the staff of his old age a staff of the spirit and adds to the inanimate temple a living temple.[20] To this most beautiful and heavenly edifice he adds one of any old kind and stature, yet to him most precious, which he completed with many sweats and labors. If only one could say it was also worthy of such labors! All that is his he gives to you. What magnanimity, or, to speak more truly, what love for his children! He gives you grey hairs, youth, the temple, the high priest, the testator, the heir, the discourses you have desired. And these discourses are not such as are haphazard and poured into the air and stop at the ear but are those the Spirit writes and engraves on tablets of stone, or indeed of

---

[14] 2 Cor 8.9.
[15] Phil 2.7.
[16] Rom 8.21.
[17] Matt 20.28, 16.26.
[18] Gregory the Elder.
[19] John 10.15.
[20] The church he built and his son, Gregory Nazianzen himself.

flesh,[21] not scratched onto the surface or easily effaced but inscribed into the depth, not with ink but with grace.

7   So these things are given you by this venerable Abraham, this patriarch, this honored and respected head, this dwelling place of every good, this standard of virtue, this perfection of priesthood, who today is bringing to God the willing sacrifice, his only son, the one born of the promise.[22] But as for you, offer both to God and to us a willingness to be shepherded well, abiding in a place of verdure and nurtured by waters of rest,[23] knowing the shepherd well and being known by him, and following when as a shepherd and a free man he calls you through the door, but not following a stranger[24] who trespasses into the front courtyard as a thief and a conspirator, nor hearing a strange voice that would steal the flock by stealth and scatter it away from the truth in mountains and deserts and chasms and places that the Lord does not visit, and lead it away from the sound faith, that is faith in Father and Son and Holy Spirit, the one divinity and power—to this teaching my sheep have always listened, and may they always listen—and whose falsified and corrupted words would lead it captive and tear it away from the first and true Shepherd. From these words may we all be far, both shepherd and flock, as from toxic and deadly grass, as we are led to pasture and lead to pasture, that we all may be one[25] in Christ Jesus, now and unto the repose hereafter. To him be glory and sovereignty unto the ages. Amen.

[21]2 Cor 3.2–3.
[22]Gen 22.2, Gal 3.16.
[23]Ps 22.2, LXX.
[24]John 10.7–8.
[25]John 17.21.

On the Nativity of Christ

1   Christ is born, give glory; Christ is from the heavens, go to meet him; Christ is on earth, be lifted up. "Sing to the Lord, all the earth,"[1] and, to say both together, "Let the heavens be glad and let the earth rejoice,"[2] for the heavenly one is now earthly.[3] Christ is in the flesh, exult with trembling[4] and joy; trembling because of sin, joy because of hope. Christ comes from a Virgin; women, practice virginity, that you may become mothers of Christ. Who would not worship the one "from the beginning"?[5] Who would not glorify "the Last"?[6]

2   Again the darkness is dissolved, again the light is established,[7] again Egypt is punished by darkness.[8] Again Israel is illumined by a pillar.[9] Let the people sitting in the darkness of ignorance see a great light[10] of knowledge. "The old things have passed; behold, all things have become new."[11] The letter withdraws, the spirit advances;[12] the shadows have been surpassed,[13] the truth has entered after them. Melchizedek is completed, the motherless one becomes fatherless;

[1] Ps 96.1.
[2] Ps 96.11.
[3] 1 Cor 15.47.
[4] Ps 2.11.
[5] 1 John 1.1.
[6] Rev 1.17, 2.8.
[7] Gen 1.3–4.
[8] Exod 10.21–22.
[9] Exod 13.21.
[10] Isa 9.2.
[11] 2 Cor 5.17.
[12] 2 Cor 3.6.
[13] Rom 13.12.

he was motherless first, fatherless second.[14] The laws of nature are dissolved. The world above must be filled. Christ commands, let us not resist. "All nations, clap your hands,"[15] "for to us a child is born, and to us a son is given, the power is on his shoulder," for he is lifted up along with the cross, and he is called by the name "angel of great counsel," that of the Father.[16] Let John proclaim, "Prepare the way of the Lord."[17] I myself will proclaim the power of this day. The fleshless one takes flesh, the Word is made coarse, the invisible one is seen, the impalpable one is touched, the timeless one makes a beginning, the Son of God becomes Son of Man,[18] "Jesus Christ, the same yesterday and today and for the ages."[19] Let Jews be scandalized, let Greeks mock,[20] let heretics talk till their tongues ache. They will believe when they see him ascend into heaven,[21] and if not then, at least when they see him coming from heaven[22] and sitting as judge.[23]

3 These things come later. Now is the feast of the Theophany, and so also of the Nativity; for it is called both, since two names are ascribed to one reality. For God appeared to human beings through birth. On the one hand he is and is eternally from the eternal Being, above cause and principle, for there was no principle higher than the Principle. On the other hand for us he later comes into being, that the one who has given us being might also grant us well-being; or rather that, as we fell from well-being through evil, he might bring us back again to himself through incarnation. The name is Theophany, since he has appeared, and Nativity, since he has been born.

---

[14]Heb 7.3.
[15]Ps 47.1.
[16]Isa 9.6.
[17]Matt 3.3.
[18]Literally, "Son of a human being."
[19]Heb 13.8.
[20]1 Cor 1.23.
[21]John 6.62.
[22]1 Thess 4.16.
[23]Matt 25.31.

4 This is our festival, this is the feast we celebrate today, in which God comes to live with human beings, that we may journey toward God, or return—for to speak thus is more exact—that laying aside the old human being we may be clothed with the new,[24] and that as in Adam we have died so we may live in Christ,[25] born with Christ and crucified with him,[26] buried with him[27] and rising with him.[28] For it is necessary for me to undergo the good turnaround, and as painful things came from more pleasant things, so out of painful things more pleasant things must return. "For where sin abounded, grace superabounded,"[29] and if the taste [of forbidden fruit] condemned,[30] how much more does the Passion of Christ justify? Therefore we celebrate the feast not like a pagan festival but in a godly manner, not in a worldly way but in a manner above the world. We celebrate not our own concerns but the one who is ours, or rather what concerns our Master, things pertaining not to sickness but to healing, not to the first molding[31] but to the remolding.

5 And how will this be? Let us not put wreaths on our front doors, or assemble troupes of dancers, or decorate the streets. Let us not feast the eyes, or mesmerize the sense of hearing, or make effeminate the sense of smell, or prostitute the sense of taste, or gratify the sense of touch. These are ready paths to evil, and entrances of sin. Let us not be softened by delicate and extravagant clothing, whose beauty is its inutility, or by the transparency of stones, or the brilliance of gold, or the artificiality of colors that falsify natural beauty and are invented in opposition to the [divine] image; nor by "revelries and drunkenness," to which I know "debauchery and licentiousness"

[24]Eph 4.22–24.
[25]1 Cor 15.22.
[26]Gal 2.19.
[27]Rom 6.4, Col 2.12.
[28]Eph 2.6.
[29]Rom 5.20.
[30]Gen 2.17, 3.6–7.
[31]Gen 2.7.

are linked,[32] since from bad teachers come bad teachings, or rather from evil seeds come evil harvests. Let us not build high beds of straw, making shelters for the debauchery of the stomach. Let us not assess the bouquet of wines, the concoctions of chefs, the great cost of perfumes. Let earth and sea not bring us as gifts the valued dung, for this is how I know to evaluate luxury. Let us not strive to conquer each other in dissoluteness. For to me all that is superfluous and beyond need is dissoluteness, particularly when others are hungry and in want, who are of the same clay and the same composition as ourselves.[33]

6 But let us leave these things to the [pagan] Greeks and to Greek pomps and festivals. They name as gods those who enjoy the steam rising from the fat of sacrificed animals and correspondingly serve the divine with their stomachs, and they become evil fashioners and initiators and initiates of evil demons. But if we, for whom the Word is an object of worship, must somehow have luxury, let us have as our luxury the word and the divine law and narratives, especially those that form the basis of the present feast, that our luxury may be akin and not foreign to the one who has called us.

Would you like me—for I am your host today—to set before you, my good guests, a discourse as abundant and lavish as possible, that you may know how a stranger can feed the local inhabitants, and a rustic the city dwellers, and one without luxury the luxurious, and one poor and homeless those brilliant in wealth? I will begin from this point; and purify for me your mind and hearing and thoughts, you who enjoy luxuries of this kind, since the discourse is about God and divine things, that you may depart having truly received the luxuries that are not empty. This discourse will be at the same time very full and very concise, so as neither to sadden you by its poverty nor cause distaste through satiety.

[32]Rom 13.13.
[33]Gen 2.7.

7 God always was and is and will be, or rather always "is," for "was" and "will be" belong to our divided time and transitory nature; but he is always "he who is," and he gave himself this name when he consulted with Moses on the mountain.[34] For holding everything together in himself, he possesses being, neither beginning nor ending. He is like a kind of boundless and limitless sea of being, surpassing all thought and time and nature. He is only sketched by the mind, and this in a very indistinct and mediocre way, not from things pertaining to himself but from things around him. Impressions are gathered from here and there into one particular representation of the truth, which flees before it is grasped and escapes before it is understood. It illumines the directive faculty in us, when indeed we have been purified, and its appearance is like a swift bolt of lightning that does not remain. It seems to me that insofar as it is graspable, the divine draws [us] toward itself, for what is completely ungraspable is unhoped for and unsought. Yet one wonders at the ungraspable, and one desires more intensely the object of wonder, and being desired it purifies, and purifying it makes deiform, and with those who have become such he converses as with those close to him,—I speak with vehement boldness—God is united with gods,[35] and he is thus known, perhaps as much as he already knows those who are known to him.[36]

For the divine is without limits and difficult to contemplate, and this alone is entirely graspable in it, namely that it is without limits, whether one supposes that to be a simple nature is to be wholly ungraspable or perfectly graspable. For what is a being whose nature is simple? Let us inquire further, for simplicity is clearly not the nature of this being, just as composition alone is clearly not the nature of composite entities.

[34]Exod 3.14, LXX.
[35]Ps 82.1, 6.
[36]1 Cor 13.12.

8 The absence of limit is contemplated in two ways, with regard to the beginning and to the end, for that which is above both and is not contained between them is without limit. When the mind gazes steadfastly into the depth above, not having a place to stand and relying on the representations it has of God, from this perspective it names as "without beginning" that which is without limit and without outlet. Yet when it gazes at what is below and what is subsequent, it names it "immortal" and "indestructible"; and when it views the whole together, "eternal." For eternity is neither time nor some part of time, nor is it measurable, but what is time for us, measured by the movement of the sun, is for everlasting beings eternity, since it is coextensive with these beings, as if it were a kind of movement and interval of time.

For me this is enough reflection about God for now. For it is not the time to go beyond these things, since our concern here is not "theology" but "economy."[37] When I say "God," I mean Father and Son and Holy Spirit. The divinity is not diffused beyond these, lest we introduce a crowd of gods, but nor is it limited to fewer than these, lest we be condemned to a poverty of divinity, either Judaizing because of the monarchy or hellenizing because of the abundance. For the evil is alike in both cases, though it is found in opposites. This then is the Holy of Holies, which is veiled by the seraphim and glorified with a threefold "Holy,"[38] converging in one lordship and divinity, which another who preceded us has explained in a most beautiful and exalted way.

9 Yet it was not sufficient for goodness to be moved only in contemplation of itself, but it was necessary that the good be poured forth and spread outward, so that there would be more recipients

---

[37]Among the Greek fathers, *theologia* often refers to discussion of God in Godself. The corresponding term *oikonomia* refers to discussion of God's relations to the created world, including the divine plan of salvation through the incarnation of Jesus Christ.

[38]Isa 6.2–3.

of its benevolent activity, for this was the summit of goodness. Therefore it first thought of the angelic and heavenly powers, and the thought was action, accomplished by the Word and perfected by the Spirit. And thus were created the second radiances, the servants of the first Radiance, which are either intelligent spirits, or a kind of immaterial and bodiless fire, or some other nature as close to those just mentioned as possible. I would like to say that they are unmoved toward evil and have only the movement toward the good, since they are around God and are the first to be illumined by God; for things here below are illumined second. Yet I am persuaded to consider and say that they are not immovable but only difficult to move on account of the one who was called Lucifer[39] because of his radiance[40] but both became and is called darkness because of his pride, and the rebellious powers under him, who are fashioners of evil through their flight from the good and incite evil in us.

10 So therefore for these reasons the intelligible world was created, at least as far as I can investigate these matters, estimating great things by my small discourse. And since the first world was beautiful to God, he thought a second material and visible world, that which is composed of heaven and earth and the system and composite of realities existing between them. It is praiseworthy because of the good disposition of each thing, but more praiseworthy because of the good connectedness and harmony of the whole, as each thing is well adapted to another and all to all, into the full realization of one world. Thus God has shown that he was able to create not only a nature akin to himself but also what is entirely foreign to him. For the intelligible natures and those apprehended only by the mind are akin to the divine, but those apprehended by the senses are entirely foreign to it, and those which are entirely without life or movement are still farther removed.

[39]That is, "Light-Bearer."
[40]Isa 14.12–15.

Yet perhaps one who is excessively ardent and devoted to feasts may ask, What are these things to us? Spur on your pony toward the goal post. Investigate for us what concerns the feast and the reasons why we sit before you[41] today. Truly I will do this, even if I have begun with things a bit exalted, since my desire and my discourse have constrained me.

11   Thus far mind and sense perception, distinguished from each other in this way, remained within their own limits and bore in themselves the magnificence of the Creator Word. They silently praised the greatness of his works and were heralds sounding afar.[42] But there was not yet a blending out of both, nor a mixing of opposites, which is the distinctive sign of a greater wisdom and of divine superabundance concerning created natures, nor was the full wealth of goodness yet made known. So then wishing to manifest this, the Creator Word also makes one living creature out of both, I mean invisible and visible natures, that is the human being. And having taken the body from the matter already created, he breathed in breath from himself,[43] which is surely the intelligent soul and the image of God of which Scripture speaks.[44] The human being is a kind of second world, great in smallness, placed on the earth, another angel, a composite worshiper, a beholder of the visible creation, an initiate into the intelligible, king of things on earth, subject to what is above, earthly and heavenly, transitory and immortal, visible and intelligible, a mean between greatness and lowliness. He is at once spirit and flesh, spirit on account of grace, flesh on account of pride, the one that he might remain and glorify his Benefactor, the other that he might suffer and in suffering remember and be corrected if he has ambition for greatness. He is a living creature trained here and transferred elsewhere,

---

[41] In the early church bishops stood to preach, while the congregation sat.
[42] Ps 19.3–4.
[43] Gen 2.7.
[44] Gen 1.26–27.

and, to complete the mystery, deified through inclination toward God. For the light and the truth present in measure here bear me toward this end, to see and experience the radiance of God, which is worthy of the one who has bound me [to flesh] and will release me and hereafter will bind me in a higher manner.[45]

12 This being was placed in paradise,[46] whatever that paradise was then, honored with self-determination so that the good would belong to the one who chose it no less than to the one who provided its seeds. The human being was a cultivator of immortal plants,[47] that is perhaps divine thoughts, both the simpler and the more complete. He was naked[48] because of his simplicity and life free from artifice and far from any covering or screen, for such a condition befitted the one who existed at the beginning. God gave him a law as material on which his self-determination could work, and the law was a commandment indicating which plants he could possess and which one he was not to touch. And that was the tree of knowledge,[49] which was neither planted from the beginning in an evil way nor forbidden through envy—let the enemies of God not wag their tongues in that direction, nor imitate the serpent[50]—but would be good if possessed at the right time. For the tree is contemplation, according to my own contemplation, which is only safe for those of mature disposition to undertake; but it is not good for those who are still simpler and those greedy in their desire, just as adult food is not useful for those who are still tender and in need of milk.[51] But after the devil's envy and the woman's spiteful treatment, both what

---

[45]This sentence speaks of God uniting the soul to a body when a human person is created, separating the soul from the body at the moment of death, and reuniting them again at the final resurrection.

[46]Gen 2.8–15.
[47]Gen 2.15.
[48]Gen 2.25.
[49]Gen 2.16–17.
[50]Gen 3.1–3.
[51]1 Cor 3.2, 1 Pet 2.2.

she underwent as more tender and what she set before the man as more persuasive—alas for my weakness, for that of the first father is mine!—he forgot the commandment given him and yielded to the bitter taste.[52] And at once he came to be banished from the tree of life[53] and from paradise[54] and from God because of the evil, and was clothed in the tunics of skin,[55] that is perhaps the more coarse and mortal and rebellious flesh, and for the first time he knew his own shame and hid from God.[56] He gained a certain advantage from this; death is also the cutting off of sin, that evil might not be immortal, so the punishment becomes love for humankind. For thus, I am persuaded, God punishes.

13 The human being was first educated[57] in many ways corresponding to the many sins that sprouted from the root of evil for different reasons and at different times; by word, law, prophets, benefits, threats, blows, floods, conflagrations, wars, victories, defeats; signs from heaven, signs from the air, from earth, from sea; unexpected changes in men, cities, nations; by all this God sought zealously to wipe out evil. At the end a stronger remedy was necessary for more dreadful diseases: murders of each other, adulteries, false oaths, lusts for men, and the last and first of all evils, idolatry and the transfer of worship from the Creator to creatures.[58] Since these things required a greater help, they also obtained something greater. It was the Word of God himself, the one who is before the ages, the invisible, the ungraspable, the incorporeal, the Principle from the Principle, the light[59] from the light, the source of life[60] and immortality, the

52Gen 3.6.
53Gen 2.9, 3.24.
54Gen 3.23.
55Gen 3.21.
56Gen 3.7–8.
57Heb 12.6.
58Rom 1.25.
59John 8.12.
60John 1.4, 11.25.

imprint[61] of the archetypal beauty, the immutable seal,[62] the undistorted image,[63] the definition and explanation of his Father. He approaches his own image[64] and bears flesh because of my flesh and mingles himself with a rational soul because of my soul, purifying like by like. And in all things he becomes a human being, except sin.[65] He was conceived by the Virgin, who was purified beforehand in both soul and flesh by the Spirit,[66] for it was necessary that procreation be honored and that virginity be honored more. He comes forth, God with what he has assumed, one from two opposites, flesh and spirit, the one deifying and the other deified. O the new mixture! O the paradoxical blending! He who is[67] comes into being, and the uncreated is created, and the uncontained is contained, through the intervention of the rational soul, which mediates between the divinity and the coarseness of flesh. The one who enriches[68] becomes poor;[69] he is made poor in my flesh, that I might be enriched through his divinity. The full one[70] empties himself;[71] for he empties himself of his own glory for a short time, that I may participate in his fullness. What is the wealth of his goodness? What is this mystery concerning me? I participated in the [divine] image,[72] and I did not keep it; he participates in my flesh both to save the image and to make the flesh immortal. He shares with us a second communion, much more paradoxical than the first; then he gave us a share in what is superior, now he shares in what is inferior. This is more godlike than the first; this, to those who can understand, is more exalted.

[61]Heb 1.3.
[62]John 6.27.
[63]Col 1.15.
[64]Gen 1.26–27.
[65]Heb 4.15.
[66]Luke 1.35.
[67]Exod 3.14.
[68]Rom 10.12, 2 Cor 8.9.
[69]2 Cor 8.9.
[70]Col 2.9.
[71]Phil 2.7.
[72]Gen 1.26–27.

14   In regard to these things, what do the slanderers say to us,[73] the bitter calculators of divinity, the accusers of praiseworthy things, the dark ones speaking of the light, the uneducated speaking of wisdom, for whom "Christ died in vain,"[74] the unthankful creatures, fashioned by the Evil One? Do you bring as a charge against God his good deed? Is he small because he is humble for your sake? Do you accuse the Good Shepherd because he went to the one who strayed,[75] he who laid down his life for the sheep,[76] to find the stray "on the mountains and the hills where you offered sacrifice,"[77] and having found it took it on his shoulder,[78] on which also he carried the cross, and having taken it brought it back to the life on high, and having brought it on high counted it again among those who remained there? Do you accuse him because he lit a lamp, his own flesh, and swept the house, cleansing the world of sin, and searched for the coin,[79] the royal image covered with a heap of passions, then calls together his friends,[80] the angelic powers, once he has found the coin, and makes participants in his joy those angels initiated into the mystery of his saving plan?[81] Do you accuse him because the most radiant Light follows the lamp, his forerunner John,[82] and the Word follows the voice,[83] and the Bridegroom follows the friend of the bridegroom,[84] who prepares for the Lord a chosen people[85] and through water purifies them beforehand for the Spirit? Do you bring these charges against God? Do you also suppose that he is inferior

[73]In this paragraph and the next, Gregory contends against his anti-Nicaean opponents, responding to arguments proposed by Arians and Eunomians.
[74]Gal 2.21.
[75]Luke 15.4.
[76]John 10.11.
[77]Hos 4.13.
[78]Luke 15.5.
[79]Luke 15.8.
[80]Luke 15.9.
[81]Luke 15.8–9.
[82]John 5.35.
[83]John 1.23.
[84]Matt 3.11, 9.15; Luke 3.16, 5.34–35; John 1.26.
[85]Luke 1.17, Tit 2.14.

for these reasons, that he girds himself with a towel and washes the feet of his disciples,[86] and shows that the best way to be exalted is lowliness,[87] since he lowers himself because of the soul bent down to the ground,[88] so as also to lift up with himself those leaning downward because of sin? But how do you not accuse him because he also eats with tax collectors and at the homes of tax collectors[89] and makes tax collectors his disciples,[90] that he also may make some profit for himself? What profit? The salvation of sinners. If so, one must also blame the physician for bending over one who is ill and enduring the stench to give health to the sick; or one who through compassion leans over a pit to rescue, according to the law,[91] the animal that has fallen into it.

15 He was sent,[92] but as human, for he was twofold. For he was tired[93] and hungry[94] and thirsty[95] and endured agony[96] and wept[97] through the law of the body, but if he underwent these things also as God, what of it? Consider the good will of the Father to be sent forth, and to it the Son ascribes his own activities, both as honoring the timeless Beginning and so as not to seem to be a rival god. For indeed Scripture says that he was given up,[98] but it is also written that he gave himself up;[99] and he was raised and taken up to heaven by the Father,[100] but he also resurrected himself and ascended there

[86]John 13.4.
[87]Luke 14.11, 18.14.
[88]Matt 26.38–39, Mark 14.34–35.
[89]Matt 9.11, Luke 19.2, 7.
[90]Matt 9.9, Mark 2.14, Luke 5.27–28.
[91]Deut 22.4.
[92]John 3.34, 5.36–37, 6.40, etc.
[93]John 4.6.
[94]Matt 4.2, 21.18.
[95]John 4.7, 19.28.
[96]Luke 22.49.
[97]Luke 19.41, John 11.35.
[98]Rom 4.25, 1 Cor 11.23.
[99]Gal 2.20, Eph 5.2, 25.
[100]Acts 17.31, Rom 4.24, Mark 16.19.

again.[101] For one is the Father's good will, the other is his own power. You speak of what belittles him, but you overlook what exalts him; you recognize that he suffered, but you do not add that it was voluntary. It is as if the Word still suffers now! By some he is honored as God but confused with the Father; by others he is dishonored as flesh and separated from him. Against which is he more angry? Rather, whom must he pardon more? Those who unite Father and Son wrongly or those who divide them? For the former would need to distinguish and the latter would need to conjoin; the one in regard to number, the other in regard to divinity. Do you take offense at the flesh? So did the Jews. Do you also call him a Samaritan?[102] I will be silent about the rest. Do you disbelieve in his divinity? This even the demons do not do.[103] O you who are more unbelieving than demons and more senseless than Jews! The latter regarded "Son" as a term denoting equality of honor,[104] the former knew that God drove them out,[105] for they were persuaded by what they suffered. But you neither accept the equality nor confess the divinity. It would have been better for you to be circumcised and possessed by a demon, if I may say something ridiculous, rather than in uncircumcision and good health to be in a state of wickedness and atheism.

16   So shortly you will also see the purification of Jesus in the Jordan[106] for my purification; or rather he is cleansed for the purification of the waters, for he indeed did not need purification, who takes away the sin of the world.[107] The heavens are parted[108] and he receives the testimony of the Spirit,[109] who is akin to him. He

[101]Matt 28.6, Mark 16.9, 19.
[102]John 8.48.
[103]James 2.19.
[104]John 5.18.
[105]Mark 1.34, Luke 4.41.
[106]Matt 3.13.
[107]John 1.29.
[108]Mark 1.10, Matt 3.16.
[109]Matt 3.16, Mark 1.10, Luke 3.22, John 1.32.

is tempted and conquers the tempter and is served by angels.[110] He heals every sickness and every infirmity, and gives life to the dead.[111] Would that he would give life to you who are dead through your false doctrine. He drives out demons, some by himself[112] and others through his disciples.[113] With a few loaves he feeds tens of thousands,[114] and he walks on the sea.[115] He is betrayed[116] and crucified[117] and crucifies my sin with himself.[118] He is offered as a lamb[119] and offers as a priest,[120] he is buried as a human being,[121] raised as God,[122] then also ascends,[123] and he will return with his own glory.[124] How many celebrations there are for me corresponding to each of the mysteries of Christ! Yet they all have one completion, my perfection[125] and refashioning and restoration to the state of the first Adam.

17 Now welcome for me his conception and leap for joy, if not indeed like John in the womb,[126] then like David when the ark came to rest.[127] Be awed at the census record through which you have been recorded in heaven, and revere the birth through which you have been released from the bonds of birth, and honor little Bethlehem, which has brought you back to paradise, and bow before the manger

[110]Matt 4.1–11, Mark 1.12–13, Luke 4.1–13.
[111]Matt 9.25; Mark 5.41; Luke 8.54–55, 7.14–15; John 11.43–44.
[112]Matt 8.16 and elsewhere.
[113]Matt 10.8, Mark 6.13, Luke 9.1, 10.17.
[114]Matt 14.16–21 and parallels.
[115]Matt 14.25, Mark 6.48, John 6.19.
[116]Matt 26.47–49, Mark 14.43–45, Luke 22.47–49, John 18.2.
[117]Matt 27.35, Mark 15.24, Luke 23.33, John 19.17.
[118]Col 2.14.
[119]Isa 53.7, Jer 11.19.
[120]Ps 109.4, Heb 7.17.
[121]Matt 27.60, Mark 15.46, Luke 23.53, John 19.41–42.
[122]Matt 28.6, Mark 16.6, Luke 24.7.
[123]Mark 16.19, Luke 24.51, Acts 1.9–10.
[124]Acts 1.11.
[125]Heb 2.10.
[126]Luke 1.41.
[127]2 Sam 6.14.

through which you who were without reason have been fed by the Word. Know, like the ox, your owner—Isaiah exhorts you[128]—and like the donkey know your master's crib, whether you are among those who are pure and under the law and chew the cud of the Word and are prepared for sacrifice, or whether up to now you are among the impure and unfit for food or sacrifice and belong to the Gentiles. Run after the star, and bring gifts with the magi, gold and frankincense and myrrh, as to a king and a God and one dead for your sake. With the shepherds give glory, with the angels sing hymns, with the archangels dance. Let there be a common celebration of the heavenly and earthly powers. For I am persuaded that they rejoice and celebrate with us today, if indeed they love humankind and love God, just as David represents them ascending with Christ after his Passion as they come to meet him and exhort each other to lift up the gates.[129]

18   You should hate only one of the events surrounding the birth of Christ, Herod's murder of children; but rather, revere this sacrifice of those of the same age as Christ, who are sacrificed before the new victim. If he flees to Egypt, be willingly banished with him. It is good to flee with the persecuted Christ. If Christ delays in Egypt, call him forth from Egypt, where he is worshiped well.[130] Travel blamelessly through all the stages of Christ's life and all his powers, as a disciple of Christ. Be purified, be circumcised, that is remove the veil that has surrounded you since birth. After this teach in the temple, drive out the traders in divine things,[131] be stoned if it is necessary that you suffer this; you will escape from those throwing the stones, I

[128]Isa 1.3.

[129]Ps 24.7–10.

[130]Gregory alludes to the fact that at the time of this homily Archbishop Peter of Alexandria and his church remain loyal to the faith of Nicaea and the memory of Athanasius, but great controversy still surrounds Nicaean doctrine in Constantinople.

[131]Matt 21.12.

know well, and you will flee through the midst of them like God.[132] For the Word is not stoned. If you are brought before Herod, do not answer for the most part. He will revere your silence more than the long discourses of others. If you are scourged, seek the other tortures. Taste the gall because of the taste [of the forbidden fruit]. Drink the vinegar, seek the spittings, accept the blows, the beatings; be crowned with thorns through the harshness of a life in accord with God. Put on the scarlet robe, accept the reed, and the worship of those who mock the truth. Finally, be crucified with him, die with him, be buried with him willingly, so as also to be resurrected with him and glorified with him and reign with him, seeing God as far as is possible and being seen by him, who is worshiped and glorified in the Trinity, whom even now we pray to be manifest to us as clearly as is possible to prisoners of the flesh, in Christ Jesus our Lord, to whom be glory and sovereignty unto the ages of ages. Amen.

[132]John 8.59, Luke 4.30. Once during his "underground" ministry at the house church in Constantinople, before Theodosius arrived in the city and restored the Nicaean faith, Gregory's enemies burst in during a service and attempted to stone him.

On the Baptism of Christ

1 Again my Jesus, and again a mystery, a mystery not deceitful or disorderly, nor belonging to the disorder and drunkenness of the [pagan] Greeks—for thus I name their solemnities, as, I think, everyone sensible will—but a mystery exalted and divine and bringing the radiance from above. For the holy day of lights, to which we have come and which we are deemed worthy to celebrate today, takes its origin from the baptism of my Christ, the true light, which illumines every human being coming into the world,[1] effects my purification, and strengthens the light we received from him from the beginning, which we darkened and blotted out through sin.

2 Therefore listen to the divine voice, which resounds very strongly in me, the initiate and the initiator of these mysteries; and may it also resound in you: "I am the light of the world."[2] And because of this "come near to him and be illumined and your faces will not be ashamed,"[3] being marked with the sign of the true light.[4] It is the time of rebirth; let us be born from above. It is the time of refashioning; let us receive again the first Adam.[5] Let us not remain what we are but become what we once were. "The light shines in the darkness" of this life and the flesh, and it is persecuted by the darkness but not overcome,[6] I mean by the adverse power, who out of

[1] John 1.9.
[2] John 8.12.
[3] Ps 34.5.
[4] John 1.9.
[5] 1 Cor 15.45.
[6] John 1.5.

shamelessness leapt upon the visible Adam[7] but encountered God and was defeated, so that we, putting aside the darkness,[8] may draw near to the light,[9] and thus become perfect light, children of perfect light.[10] Do you see the grace of this day? Do you see the power of the mystery? Have you not been lifted up from the earth? Have you not clearly been placed above, exalted by our voice and our guidance upward? And you will be placed still higher when the Word has guided this discourse well.

3 Is it some kind of legal and shadowy purification, providing aid through temporary sprinklings and sprinkling the ashes of a heifer on those who have become unclean?[11] Is it something like what the Greeks reveal in their initiations? To me all their initiations and mysteries are nonsense, dark inventions of demons and fabrications of a demon-possessed mind, assisted by time and deceived by myth. For what they worship as true they hide as mythical. If these things are true, they should not call them myths but show that they are not shameful; if false, they should not marvel, nor so recklessly hold opposite opinions about the same subject. It is as if they were playing in the marketplace with children, or rather with truly demon-possessed men, and not conversing with men of reason who worship the Word though they spit upon this contrived and sordid plausibility.

4. With us there are no births and thefts of Zeus, the Cretan tyrant, though the Greeks are displeased; nor Curetes shouting and clapping and dancing with their weapons, drowning out the noise of a crying god, so as to hide him from a father who hates children; for it would have been strange for one swallowed as a stone to cry as a child.[12] Nor the Phrygians' mutilations and flutes and Corybantes,

[7]That is, Christ.
[8]Rom 13.12.
[9]John 3.21.
[10]Eph 5.8.
[11]Heb 9.13.
[12]Gregory refers to stories of the birth and childhood of Zeus, whose father

nor all the people's ravings about Rhea, initiating others into the cult of the mother of the gods and being initiated as befits the mother of such gods.[13] Nor for us is there any maiden abducted, nor does Demeter wander or introduce any Cerei and Triptolemoi and dragons or things she does and suffers. For I am ashamed to grant to the day the initiation of the night and make what is unseemly a mystery. Eleusis knows these things, as do those who see the things that are guarded in silence and are surely deserving of silence.[14] Nor is there Dionysus or the thigh in labor with an unformed fetus, as formerly a head was with another one;[15] nor the androgynous god and the drunken chorus and the relaxed army and the Theban madness honoring this god and the thunderbolt of Semele that is worshipped.[16] Nor the harlot mysteries of Aphrodite, who, as they say themselves, was shamefully born and is shamefully honored. Nor any Phalloi and Ithyphalloi, shameful both as images and as objects;[17] nor Taurian murders of strangers,[18] nor blood of Lacedemonian youths on the altar, as they are scourged with the whips and in this alone are

Kronos learned that one of his children would dethrone him and tried to eat them all. His wife Rhea saved Zeus by substituting a stone for the baby and taking him to Crete, where warriors named Curetes protected him. Worshipers re-enacted this story by dancing and shouting like the warriors so the child's murderous father would not hear him cry and find him.

[13]The Corybantes of Phrygia worshipped Rhea with ecstatic dancing and mutilated themselves with small knives.

[14]In Greece the Eleusinian Mysteries, whose initiates guarded its secrets in silence, celebrated the renewal of vegetation and grain through the myth of Demeter and her daughter Kore, who was abducted and taken to the underworld. Demeter endures many wanderings and sufferings as she searches for her lost child.

[15]Athena was born from the head of Zeus. Zeus fathered Dionysus by his lover Semele, and when she died during pregnancy enclosed the fetus in his thigh until it came to term.

[16]Dionysus was thought to have both masculine and feminine qualities. His worship involved drunkenness and sexual license. It was thought that Zeus struck Semele with a thunderbolt.

[17]Aphrodite was the Greek goddess of sexual desire, and she was worshipped by dancers carrying phallic symbols.

[18]The playwright Euripides tells a story of strangers being killed and sacrificed to the goddess Artemis at a temple in Taurus.

manly in a bad way, who honor a goddess, one who is a virgin. For they both honored effeminacy and revered boldness.[19]

5   And where will you place the butchery of Pelops, who provides a feast to hungry gods and his cruel and inhuman hospitality?[20] Where will you place the frightening and nocturnal phantoms of Hekate, and the subterranean games and oracles of Trophanius, and the gibberish of the oak of Dordona, and the fallacies of the tripod of Delphi, and the prophetic drink of Castalia?[21] This alone they could not prophesy, their own silence. Nor is there the sacrificial skill of the magi and their predictions through cutting victims, nor the astronomy of the Chaldeans and their horoscopes that connect our affairs with the movements of the heavens, who themselves are unable to understand what they are or will be.[22] Nor are there those Thracian orgies, from which, they say, come the word for "worship";[23] nor the initiations and mysteries of Orpheus, at whom the Greeks marveled so much for his wisdom that they also made for him a lyre that draws all things by its music;[24] nor the just punishment of Mithras against those who accept to be initiated into such mysteries;[25] nor the tearing apart of Osiris, another disaster honored by the Egyptians; nor the misfortunes of Isis[26] and the goats more venerable than the

[19]The Spartans, also known as Lacedemonians, honored Artemis with an initiation ritual in which boys whipped each other until they bled.

[20]A myth tells of how Tantalus prepared a feast for visiting gods by butchering, cooking, and serving them his son Pelops.

[21]Here Gregory refers to several well known pagan oracles and forms of prophesy.

[22]The magi—three of whom visited the infant Christ, as Matthew tells the story—were Zoroastrian priests, astronomers and astrologers, and also foretold the future by examining the entrails of sacrificed animals. The Chaldeans also practiced astronomy and astrology, which were studied together in the ancient world and only later became clearly separate disciplines.

[23]The Greek word is *threskeuein*, hence the pun or supposed etymology linking it to Thrace.

[24]Orpheus was a musician whose playing was thought to charm all of nature.

[25]Mithras was a sun god from Persia worshipped throughout the Roman world, especially by soldiers. Initiation in his cult was expensive, strenuous and dangerous.

[26]Osiris, according to Egyptian myth, was cut into pieces by his brother Typho.

Mendesians and the feeding trough of Apis, the calf feasting on the foolishness of the Memphites;[27] nor those honors by which they insult the Nile,[28] while themselves singing its praises as giver of fruit and rich in grain and measuring happiness by its cubits.

6 For I do not speak of the honors given to reptiles and beasts and the emulation of impropriety, none of which have any initiation or festival of their own. Yet all share a common demonic possession. So if indeed they absolutely had to be ungodly and fall away from the glory of God,[29] bowing down to idols and works of art and things made by hands, sensible people could not wish anything worse for themselves than to venerate such things and to honor them in such a way, "that they might receive the recompense due for their error," as Paul says,[30] in the things they venerate. They do not honor through themselves the things they venerate as much as they are dishonored by them. They are abominable because of their error, more abominable because of the vileness of the things they worship and venerate, so that they are more lacking in perception than the very objects they honor, being more exceedingly foolish than the things they worship are vile.

7 So let the children of the Greeks play with these things, and the demons from whom their foolishness has come, who draw aside God's honor to themselves and divide people in various ways into shameful opinions and fantasies. For they have expelled us from the tree of life[31] by means of the tree of knowledge[32] partaken of inappropriately at the wrong time, then overrun us since we were

Isis, the wife of Osiris, had to search for all the pieces and reassemble them.

[27]In Egypt, the people of Mendes worshipped a god in the form of a goat, and those in Memphis worshipped Apis in the form of a calf.

[28]Egyptians considered the Nile almost a god, since its annual flooding made possible the agriculture on which the country depended for life and prosperity.

[29]Rom 3.23.

[30]Rom 1.27, 6.23.

[31]Gen 3.22–24.

[32]Gen 2.9–17.

weaker than before, carrying away completely our guide, the mind, and opening a door to the passions. For since they are by nature envious and hate humankind—or rather became such because of their own wickedness—they could not bear those below attaining things on high, since they themselves fell to earth from above, nor could they bear the occurrence of such a transformation of humans' glory and first nature. This is the persecution of the one molded,[33] through this the image of God[34] is outraged; and as we did not see fit to keep the commandment[35] we have been given over to the self-rule of error, and as we have erred we have been dishonored by the things we venerated. For there was not only this disaster, that having been made for good works to his glory and praise and having been made to imitate God as far as is possible, we have become a base of operations for all kinds of passions, which devour horribly and consume the inner human being;[36] but also we have set up the gods as advocates of the passions, so that sin is regarded not only as blameless but even as divine, since it appeals to this defense, the things worshipped.

8 As for us, as indeed we have been given grace to flee the error of superstition, be joined to the truth and serve the living and true God,[37] and to rise above the creation, passing beyond everything subject to time and the first motion, so also let us know and reflect on the things around God and divine things. As we begin, let us reflect on where it is better to begin; and it is better where Solomon legislated for us. "The beginning of wisdom," he says, "is to acquire wisdom."[38] What does he mean by this "beginning of wisdom"? Fear.[39] For one must not begin from contemplations and end in

[33]Gen 2.7.
[34]Gen 1.26–27.
[35]Gen 2.16–17.
[36]Eph 3.16.
[37]Heb 9.14.
[38]Prov 4.7.
[39]Sir 1.16.

fear—for unbridled contemplation would perhaps push us down precipices—but let us be set straight and purified by fear and, if I may speak thus, made light so as to rise on high. For where there is fear there is keeping of commandments; and where there is keeping of commandments there is purification of the flesh, that cloud covering the soul and not allowing one to see purely the divine ray; and where there is purification there is illumination. And illumination is the fulfillment of desire for those who aim for the greatest things, or that which is greatest, or that which is beyond greatness.

9   Because of this, let us each first purify ourselves, then come close to the pure, if indeed we do not want what Israel experienced, not bearing the glory of Moses' face and because of this needing a veil,[40] or again what Manoah experienced, so that he said, "We are lost, wife, we have seen God," as God appeared to him;[41] or like Peter, to send away Jesus from the boat, as not worthy of such a visit.[42] And when I say Peter, of whom do I speak? The one who walked on the waves.[43] Or, like Paul, to be stricken in the eyes, when before being purified of persecuting he came close to the one he persecuted, or rather to a brief flash of the great light;[44] or, like the centurion to seek healing, but because of praiseworthy fear not receive the healer into his house.[45] Let such of us also, as long as he is not yet purified, but is still a centurion ruling many in evil, and serves as a soldier for Caesar the world ruler of those dragged downward, say, "I am not sufficient for you to come under my roof."[46] But when he has seen Jesus, though he was small in spiritual stature like the renowned Zaccheus[47] and has climbed atop the sycamore tree, mortifying his

[40]Exod 34.30–35.
[41]Judg 13.22.
[42]Luke 5.8.
[43]Matt 14.28–29.
[44]Acts 9.1–18.
[45]Matt 8.5–10.
[46]Matt 8.10.
[47]Luke 19.2–10.

limbs upon the earth[48] and mounting above the body of lowliness,[49] then indeed let him receive the word and hear, "Today salvation has come to this house,"[50] and let him receive salvation and bear the more mature fruits, pouring forth and dispersing well what he has gathered badly as a tax collector.[51]

10　For the same Word is both fearful because of his nature to those who are not worthy and graspable because of his love for humankind to those who are thus prepared, who have driven out the impure and material spirit from their souls and swept clean and adorned their own souls by full knowledge,[52] and not let them be idle or inactive so as to be seized again with greater power by the seven spirits of wickedness,[53] whose number equals that of the virtues.[54] For what is hardest to fight calls for more effort. But to flight from vice they add practice of virtue, bringing to dwell within themselves the whole Christ, or as much of him as possible, so that the wicked power does not encounter any empty place to fill again with himself, and the last state does not become worse than the first[55] through the greater vehemence of the attack and because the fortress is more secure and more difficult to capture. When we have "guarded our own soul with all vigilance"[56] and "arranged ascents in our heart,"[57] and "broken up our fallow ground"[58] and "sown unto righteousness,"[59] as Solomon and David and Jeremiah advise, let us light in ourselves the light of knowledge. Then let us speak of the wisdom of God hidden in a

[48]Col 3.5.
[49]Phil 3.21.
[50]Luke 19.9.
[51]Luke 19.8.
[52]Matt 12.44, Luke 11.25.
[53]Matt 12.45, Luke 11.26.
[54]Isa 11.2, LXX.
[55]Matt 12.45, Luke 11.26.
[56]Prov 4.23.
[57]Ps 84.5.
[58]Jer 4.3.
[59]Hos 10.12.

mystery[60] and illumine others. Meanwhile, let us purify ourselves and be initiated beforehand into the Word, that we may work the most good possible for ourselves, making ourselves deiform, and receive the Word who is coming; and not only this but also hold him fast and manifest him to others.

11 Since we have purified the place of this assembly by our discourse, come now, let us reflect a little about the feast, and celebrate with the souls that love feasts and love God. And since the main point of the feast is the remembrance of God, let us remember God. For indeed the sound of those celebrating there, where there is the dwelling of all who rejoice,[61] I consider to be nothing other than this, hymning and glorifying God by those counted worthy of the citizenship there. And if the present discourse contains some things I have said before, let no one marvel. For I will not only utter the same words, but also speak about the same realities, trembling both in tongue and mind when I speak of God and praying that you also may have the same praiseworthy and blessed experience. When I speak of God, be struck from all sides by the lightning flash of one light and also three; three in regard to the individualities, that is hypostases, if one prefers to call them this, or persons, for we will not struggle with our comrades about the names as long as the syllables convey the same idea; but one if one speaks of the essence, that is the divinity. For they are divided undividedly, if I may speak thus, and united in division. For the divinity is one in three, and the three are one, in whom the divinity is, or, to speak more precisely, who are the divinity. But we omit the excesses and omissions, neither making the union a fusion, nor the division a separation. Let both the contraction of Sabellius and the division of Arius be equally far from us, the evils that are diametrically opposed yet equal in impiety. For why is it necessary to either fuse God together wrongly or cut him up into inequalities?

[60] 1 Cor 2.7.
[61] Ps 87.7.

12 "But for us there is one God, the Father, from whom are all things, and one Lord, Jesus Christ, through whom are all things,"[62] and one Holy Spirit, in whom are all things, yet the "from whom" and "through whom" and "in whom" do not divide natures—for then neither would the prepositions change, nor the order of the nouns—but they characterize the properties of a nature that is one and unconfused. And this is clear from the fact that they are again brought together into one, if these other words of the same apostle are not read as an afterthought: "from whom and through whom and in whom are all things; to him be the glory unto the ages. Amen."[63] The Father is a father and without origin, for he is not from anyone. The Son is a son and not without origin, for he is from the Father. But if you take it to mean an origin in time, he is also without origin; for he is Creator of time, not subject to time. The Holy Spirit is truly the Spirit sent forth from the Father, yet not as a son or through begetting but through procession, if indeed one must make some innovation in words for the sake of clarity. Nor does the Father cease to be unbegotten because he has begotten, nor does the Son cease to be begotten since he is from the unbegotten—how could that be?— nor does the Spirit change either into the Father or into the Son because he proceeds or because he is God, though to the godless this does not seem to be so; for the property does not shift. For how could it remain a property if it were shifted and changed? Those who consider that "unbegotten" and "begotten" name natures of gods would perhaps also consider that Adam and Seth are separate from each other in regard to nature, since the one was not born from flesh but molded by God[64] while the other was born from Adam and Eve.[65] So there is one God in three, and the three are one as indeed we have said.

[62]1 Cor 8.6.
[63]Rom 11.36.
[64]Gen 2.7.
[65]Gen 4.25.

13 And since these realities are thus, or this reality, it was necessary that the worship not be limited only to those above, but that there be some worshipers also below, that all things may be filled with the glory of God, since indeed all are of God. For this reason the human being was created, honored with the hand of God and his image.[66] But to neglect this creature, who by the envy of the devil and the bitter taste of sin[67] is pitiably separated from God his Creator, is not God's way. What happens? And what is the great mystery concerning us? An innovation is made to natures, and God becomes human, and he who "has mounted upon the heaven of heavens at the dawn"[68] of his own glory and splendor, is glorified at the sunset of our cheapness and lowliness, and the Son of God accepts both to become Son of a human being and to be called such; not changing what he was, for he is immutable, but assuming what he was not, for he loves humankind, that the ungraspable might be grasped, associating with us through the mediation of flesh, as if through a covering, since his pure divinity cannot be borne by a nature subject to generation and corruption. For this reason unmingled realities are mingled, not only God with generation, or mind with flesh, or the atemporal with time, or the uncircumscribed with measure, but also childbirth with virginity, and dishonor with what is above all honor, and suffering with the impassible, and the immortal with the corruptible. For since the deceptive advocate of evil thought he was unconquerable as he ensnared us with the hope of divinity,[69] he was ensnared by the obstacle of flesh. Just as when he meant to attack Adam he encountered God, so also by the new Adam the old was saved[70] and the condemnation of the flesh was abolished,[71] since death was put to death by flesh.

---

[66]Gen 2.7, 1.26–27.
[67]Gen 3.6.
[68]Ps 68.33.
[69]Gen 3.5.
[70]1 Cor 15.35.
[71]Rom 5.16–18.

14 Therefore at his birth we kept festival as was fitting, both I the leader of the feast, and you, and all that is in the world and above the world. With the star we ran, and with the magi we worshipped,[72] and with the shepherds we were surrounded by light, and with the angels we gave glory.[73] With Symeon we took him in our arms, and with aged and chaste Anna we gave thanks.[74] And thanks be to the one who came to his own as a stranger,[75] that he might glorify his host. But now there is another deed of Christ and another mystery. I cannot hold back my joy, I become inspired, and almost like John I announce the good news,[76] if not indeed as a forerunner, at least from the desert. Christ is illumined,[77] let us flash like lightning with him. Christ is baptized,[78] let us go down with him, that we may also come up again with him. Jesus is baptized. Is this all? Or is it necessary also to attend carefully to the other matters? Who is he? And by whom is he baptized? And when? The pure one, and by John, and at the beginning of his signs.[79] What are we to learn and what are we to be taught by this? To purify ourselves beforehand, and to be humble minded, and to preach when mature both in spiritual and bodily stature. The first lesson is addressed to those who rush to baptism precipitously and do not prepare beforehand or assure the security of their redemption through a disposition toward the good. For indeed if the grace entails release from what is past, for it is grace, now, still more, reverent fear is fitting, lest we return again to

[72]Matt 2.8–11.

[73]Luke 2.9–14.

[74]Luke 2.28–38. This reference implies that at 380 the encounter with Symeon and Anna takes place at Christmas, not yet at the Feast of the Meeting of Our Lord (February 2nd). Between 381 and 384, according to Egeria, this feast was celebrated at Jerusalem. It spread from there to Antioch (ca. 513–518) and Constantinople (534). See Kenneth W. Stevenson, "The Origins and Development of Candlemas: A Struggle for Identity and Coherence?" in J. Neil Alexander, ed., *Time and Community: In Honor of Thomas Justin Talley* (Washington, DC: Pastoral Press, 1990), 43–73, 49–53.

[75]John 1.11.

[76]Matt 3.1, Mark 1.4, Luke 3.3.

[77]In the early church, "illumination" was another name for baptism.

[78]Matt 3.13, Mark 1.9, Luke 3.21.

[79]John 2.11.

our own vomit.[80] The next is addressed to those who rise up against those who dispense the mysteries, if in any way they surpass them in rank. The third is addressed to those who are overconfident in youth and consider that every time is appropriate for teaching or presiding. Jesus is purified, and you despise purification? By John, and you rebel against your herald? He was thirty years old,[81] and you, before you have a beard, teach the elders, or believe you can teach, though you are not revered because of age, or perchance because of character? Here one speaks of Daniel,[82] or this one or that one, young judges, and the examples are on your tongue. For all the guilty are ready with a defense. But the exception is not the law of the Church, if indeed one swallow does not make a summer, nor one line a geometer, nor one voyage a sailor.

15 Yet as John is baptizing, Jesus approaches, perhaps also to sanctify the baptizer, and certainly to bury all the old Adam[83] in the water, but before these things and for the sake of these things to sanctify the Jordan. As indeed he was spirit and flesh, so he initiates by the Spirit and the water. The baptizer does not accept it; Jesus debates [with him]. "I need to be baptized by you,"[84] the lamp[85] says to the sun,[86] the voice[87] to the Word, the friend[88] to the bridegroom, the one above all born of women[89] to the first born of all creation,[90] the one who leaped in the womb[91] to the one worshiped in the womb, the one who was and will be the Forerunner[92] to the one who was

[80]Prov 26.11, 2 Pet 2.22.
[81]Luke 3.23.
[82]Sus 45–50.
[83]1 Cor 15.45.
[84]Matt 3.14.
[85]John 5.35.
[86]Mal 4.2.
[87]Matt 3.3, Mark 1.3, Luke 3.4.
[88]John 3.29, Matt 9.15.
[89]Matt 11.11, Luke 7.28.
[90]Col 1.15.
[91]Luke 1.41.
[92]Matt 11.10, Mark 1.2, Luke 7.27.

and will be made manifest. "I need to be baptized by you"; add "and for you." For he knew that he would be baptized by martyrdom or, like Peter, would not have only his feet cleansed.[93] "And you come to me?"[94] This is also prophetic. For he knew that after the madness of Herod would come that of Pilate,[95] so as he himself departed beforehand, Christ would follow. But what does Jesus say? "Let it be so now";[96] for this is the divine plan. For he knew that shortly he himself would baptize the baptizer. And what is the winnowing fan?[97] Purification. And what is the fire?[98] The destruction of the chaff and the fervor of the Spirit. And what is the axe?[99] The cutting down of the soul that is incurable, even after the manure.[100] And what is the sword?[101] The cut made by the Word, which divides the worse from the better, and separates believer from unbeliever, and stirs up son and daughter and bride against father and mother and mother-in-law,[102] the new and recent against the old and shadowy. And what is the fastening of the sandal, which you who baptize Jesus cannot undo,[103] you who live in the desert even without food,[104] the new Elijah,[105] the one surpassing the prophets,[106] to the extent that you have seen what they prophesied, the mediator of the old and the new covenants? What is it? Perhaps the principle of Christ's sojourn and the flesh, a matter that is not easy to solve even apart from the

[93]John 13.6–8.
[94]Matt 3.14.
[95]Matt 14.3–5, 27.26; Mark 6.17, 15.15; Luke 3.19–20, 23.24–25; John 19.16.
[96]Matt 3.15.
[97]Matt 3.12.
[98]Matt 3.10–12.
[99]Matt 3.10.
[100]Luke 13.8.
[101]Matt 10.34.
[102]Matt 10.35, Luke 12.53.
[103]Mark 1.7, Luke 3.16, John 1.27.
[104]Matt 3.4, Mark 1.6.
[105]Matt 11.14.
[106]Matt 11.9.

loftiest meaning, either for those who are still fleshly and infants in Christ or for those who are like John in the Spirit.

16   But Jesus comes up again out of the water.[107] For he carries up with himself the world and "sees the heavens opened"[108] which Adam closed for himself and for those after him as he also closed paradise by the flaming sword.[109] And the Spirit testifies to [Christ's] divinity,[110] for he ran toward one like himself, as does the voice from heaven,[111] for from there comes the one to whom testimony is given. And the Spirit comes as a dove,[112] for he honors the body, being seen "corporeally,"[113] since it also is God by divinization. And since long ago the dove has been accustomed to announcing the good news of the flood's end.[114] But if you judge divinity by size and weight, and for this reason the Spirit is small to you because he appears in the form of a dove, you who are small-minded about the greatest things, it is time for you also to dishonor the kingdom of heaven since it is compared to a mustard seed,[115] and instead of Jesus' greatness to prefer the adversary because he is called a great mountain[116] and leviathan[117] and king of those in the waters, while Jesus is named lamb[118] and pearl[119] and drop[120] and the like.

17   Since the feast is about baptism and it is necessary to suffer a little for the one who for us took our form and was baptized and

[107]Matt 3.16, Mark 1.10.
[108]Mark 1.10.
[109]Gen 3.24.
[110]Matt 3.16, Mark 1.10, Luke 3.22.
[111]Matt 3.17, Mark 1.11, Luke 3.22.
[112]Matt 3.16, Mark 1.10, Luke 3.22.
[113]Luke 3.22.
[114]Gen 8.11.
[115]Matt 13.31.
[116]Dan 2.45.
[117]Job 3.8.
[118]John 1.29.
[119]Matt 13.46.
[120]Ps 72.6.

crucified, come let us briefly reflect on the differences among baptisms, that we may come from there purified. Moses baptized, but in water,[121] and before this "in the cloud and in the sea."[122] But this was typological, as Paul also thinks[123]: the sea was a type of the water, the cloud of the Spirit, the manna of the bread of life,[124] the drink[125] of the divine drink.[126] John also baptized, yet no longer in a Jewish way, for he did so not only in water but also for repentance,[127] but not yet in a wholly spiritual way, for he did not add the words "in the Spirit." Jesus also baptized, but in the Spirit.[128] This is perfection. And how could he not be God, if I may digress a little, by whom you also become god? I know also a fourth baptism, that through martyrdom and blood, by which Christ himself also was baptized, and it is much more venerable than the others, insofar as it is not defiled by stains afterward. And I know yet a fifth, that of tears; but it is more laborious, received by one who each night washes his bed and his couch with tears,[129] whose bruises also stink with wickedness, who goes in mourning and with a sad face,[130] who imitates the turnaround of Manassas[131] and the humiliation of the Ninivites that brought them mercy,[132] who utters the words of the tax collector in the temple and is justified instead of the arrogant Pharisee,[133] who bends down like the Canaanite woman and seeks compassion and crumbs, the food of a dog that is very hungry.[134]

[121]Exod 17.6.
[122]1 Cor 10.1–2.
[123]1 Cor 10.3.
[124]John 6.35.
[125]1 Cor 10.4.
[126]John 6.36.
[127]Mark 1.4, Matt 3.2.
[128]Matt 3.11, 28.19; Mark 1.8; Luke 3.16.
[129]Ps 6.6.
[130]Ps 38.5–6.
[131]2 Chr 33.12–16.
[132]Jonah 3.1–10.
[133]Luke 18.13–14.
[134]Matt 15.22–27, Mark 7.25–28.

18   As for me, since I confess that I am a human being, an animal with a changeable and fluid nature, I also accept this eagerly and worship the one who has given it and share it with others, and I advance them mercy that they may obtain mercy. For I know that I myself am "clothed in weakness,"[135] and I will be measured as I have measured others.[136] But what do you say?[137] What do you legislate, you new Pharisee pure in name but not in intention, who trumpet forth to us the principles of Novatus but have the same weakness? You do not accept repentance? You do not give place to lamentations? You do not weep a tear? May you not encounter a judge such as yourself! You do not respect the lovingkindness of Jesus, who has taken our weakness and borne our diseases,[138] who has not come to the righteous but to sinners[139] that they may repent, who "desires mercy rather than sacrifice,"[140] who forgives sins seventy times seven times?[141] How blessed your exaltation would be, if it were purity and not pride making laws above what is human and destroying correction by despair. For these are alike evil: both release without self-control and condemnation without pardon; the one loosens the reins completely, while the other strangles by violence. Show me your purity and I will accept your audacity. But in fact I fear that though full of wounds you propose that they are incurable. You would not accept David repenting, for whom indeed repentance preserved the prophetic gift;[142] nor the great Peter who suffered human weakness at the Savior's suffering.[143] Yet Jesus accepted him and by the

[135]Heb 5.2

[136]Matt 7.2, Mark 4.24, Luke 6.38.

[137]From here through paragraph 19, Gregory argues against the Novatianists, a rigorist sect that originated in third-century Rome but still had adherents in Constantinople and Asia Minor at the end of the fourth century. They denied that those who committed certain serious sins after baptism could be readmitted to the church's communion following repentance. Their founder's name was actually Novatianus.

[138]Isa 53.4.

[139]Luke 5.32.

[140]Hos 6.6.

[141]Matt 18.22.

[142]2 Sam 12.13.

[143]Matt 26.70–74, Mark 14.68–71, Luke 22.57–60, John 18.17–27.

threefold question and confession healed the threefold denial.[144] Or would you not have accepted him even when he was perfected through blood? For this also is part of your craziness. You would not accept the lawbreaker in Corinth?[145] But Paul indeed made love prevail for him when he saw his correction, for this reason: "That such a person might not be swallowed up by excessive sorrow,"[146] weighed down by lack of moderation in the reproof. You do not allow young widows to marry owing to the vulnerability of their age? Yet Paul dared to allow it,[147] of whom you are quite clearly the teacher, since you have reached the fourth heaven and another paradise and have heard most unspeakable words[148] and have encompassed a larger circle for the gospel.

19   But these things were not after baptism, they say: What proof is there? Either prove it or do not condemn. But if it is uncertain, let lovingkindness have the victory. But Novatus, they say, did not accept those who fell during persecution. What do you mean by this? If they did not repent, he acted justly. I myself would not receive those who either do not bow down,[149] or not sufficiently, and do not compensate for the evil by correction; and when I receive them, I assign them the proper place. But regarding those who waste away in tears, I will not imitate him. And what law to me is the inhumanity of Novatus, who did not punish avarice, the second idolatry,[150] but condemned unchastity so bitterly, as if he were fleshless and bodiless? What do you say? Are we persuading you by these words? Come, stand with us who are human beings. "Let us magnify the Lord together."[151] Let none of you dare to say, even if he is very con-

---

[144]John 21.15–17.
[145]1 Cor 5.1.
[146]2 Cor 2.7–8.
[147]1 Tim 5.14.
[148]2 Cor 12.2–4.
[149]Isa 58.5.
[150]Eph 5.5.
[151]Ps 34.3.

fident about himself, "Do not touch me, for I am pure,"[152] and, "Who is as pure as I?" Give us also a share in your splendor. But are we not persuading you? Then we will weep for you. So let them go, if they wish, our way and the way of Christ, but if not, let them go their own way. Perhaps hereafter they will be baptized by fire, the final baptism that is more laborious and longer, that devours matter like hay and consumes all evils like the lightest things.[153]

20　But let us honor today the baptism of Christ and celebrate well, not feasting with the stomach but rejoicing spiritually. And how shall we feast? "Wash, become pure."[154] If you are "red" with sin but less than blood-red, become "white as snow";[155] but if you are scarlet and complete "men of blood,"[156] still, come to be "white as wool."[157] Be entirely purified and be pure, for nothing gives so much joy to God as the correction and salvation of the human being, for whose sake every discourse and every mystery exist, that you may become like "stars in the world,"[158] a life-giving force for other human beings; that as perfect lights standing beside the great Light, you may be initiated into the illumination hereafter, illumined with greater purity and clarity by the Trinity, from whom you have now received in measure the one ray of the one divinity, in Christ Jesus our Lord, to whom be glory to the ages of ages. Amen.

[152]Isa 65.5.
[153]1 Cor 3.12–13.
[154]Isa 1.16.
[155]Isa 1.18.
[156]Ps 5.6, 139.19.
[157]Isa 1.18.
[158]Phil 2.15.

On Baptism

1 Yesterday we celebrated the radiant Day of Lights, for indeed it was fitting that rejoicings be made for our salvation, and much more than for a wedding anniversary, a birthday or a name's day, which friends of the flesh celebrate, a coming of age, a house warming or whatever other annual occasions people observe. Today we will speak briefly about baptism and the benefits that come to us from it, though yesterday our discourse ran through it quickly. The time pressed us hard, while the speech needed to avoid surfeit. Surfeit of speech is harmful to the ears, as an excess of food is to the body. Yet it is worth your while to pay attention to what is said, and receive the discourse about such a great matter, not with indifference but eagerly, since this also is an illumination, to know the power of the mystery.

2 The word of Scripture recognizes three births for us: one from the body, one from baptism, and one from resurrection. The first takes place at night and in slavery and in passions. The second takes place in the day and in freedom and releases from passions, cutting away all the veil that has surrounded us since birth and leading us back toward the life on high. The third is more fearful and more swift, assembling in a moment all that has been created and presenting it to the Creator to give an account of its servitude and way of life here, as to whether one has followed only the flesh, or risen up with the Spirit and respected the grace of the re-creation. It is manifest that my Christ has honored in himself all these births, the first by breathing in the first and living breath,[1] the second by his incarna-

[1]Gen 2.7.

tion[2] and the baptism with which he was baptized,[3] the third by the resurrection that he offered as firstfruits[4] when he became firstborn among many brothers[5] and thus deigned to become firstborn from the dead.[6]

3   About two of the births, I mean the first and the last, I will not reflect at the present time; about the middle one indeed we must now reflect, since it gives its name to the Day of Lights. This illumination[7] is radiance of souls, transformation of life, engagement of the conscience toward God.[8] Illumination is help for our weakness, illumination is renunciation of the flesh, following of the Spirit, communion in the Word, setting right of the creature, a flood overwhelming sin, participation in light, dissolution of darkness. Illumination is a vehicle[9] leading toward God, departure with Christ, support of faith, perfection of mind, key to the kingdom of heaven,[10] change of life, deliverance from slavery, release from bonds, transformation of our composite nature. Illumination—what more need I add?—is the most beautiful and most magnificent of the gifts of God. As one speaks of the Holy of Holies and the Song of Songs, since they are more comprehensive and most excellent than others, so also this is more holy that all other illuminations that we possess.

4   Just as Christ, its giver, is called by many and diverse names, so also is his gift. Either because of the great joy we experience in regard to it—for those who are very much in love with something also take pleasure in uniting themselves with its names—or because of its many forms of benefit, we have made for it many names as

[2]John 1.14.
[3]Matt 3.13–16, Mark 1.9, Luke 3.21.
[4]1 Cor 15.20–23.
[5]Rom 8.29.
[6]Col 1.18.
[7]In the early church, "illumination" is another name for baptism.
[8]1 Pet 3.21.
[9]2 Kgs 2.11.
[10]Matt 16.19.

well. We call it gift, grace, baptism, illumination, anointing, robe of
incorruption, bath of rebirth, seal, everything honorable. It is a gift
because no offering is given for it beforehand; and grace, as given
even to debtors;[11] and baptism, as burying sin in the water;[12] and
anointing, as priestly and royal,[13] since they were the ones anointed;
and illumination, as most radiant; and robe, as entirely covering
shame; and bath, as washing clean, and seal, as a safeguard and a
sign of authority. In this the heavens rejoice together, this the angels
glorify because it is akin to their great radiance. This is an image of
the blessedness to come. We desire to sing forth its praises, but we
are not able to do so worthily.

5   The highest light is God, unapproachable and ineffable, neither
grasped by the mind nor expressed in language. It illumines every
reason-endowed nature. It is to intelligible realities what the sun is
to sense-perceptible realities. To the extent that we are purified it
appears, to the extent that it appears it is loved, to the extent that it
is loved it is again known. It both contemplates and comprehends
itself and is poured out but a little to those outside itself. I speak of
the light contemplated in the Father and Son and Holy Spirit, whose
wealth is the confluence and the leaping forth of this radiance. A
second light is the angel, a kind of emanation or participation in
the first light, toward which it inclines and by whose help it possesses illumination. I do not know if the illumination is apportioned
according to the rank in which each stands, or if each receives its
rank according to the measure of its illumination. A third light is the
human being, and this is also clear to those outside the church. For
they name the human being a light because of the power of reason
in us, and in addition the name is given to those of us who are more
deiform and approach more closely to God.[14] I also know another

---

[11]Matt 6.12, Luke 11.4.
[12]Rom 6.4, Col 2.12.
[13]1 Pet 2.9.
[14]Matt 5.14, Phil 2.15.

light, by which the primordial darkness was driven away or cut off, the first thing brought into existence of the visible creation,[15] which shines upon the circular orbit of the stars and the whole universe, the beacon fire on high.[16]

6   The first precept given to the first-created human being[17] was also a light, since "the precept of the law is a lamp and light"[18] and because "your commandments are light upon the earth,"[19] although the envious darkness came in besides and fashioned evil. The written law is a light that is typological and proportionate to those receiving it, sketching the truth and the mystery of the great light, though indeed the face of Moses was also glorified by it.[20] And, to add more lights to our discourse, it was a light that appeared to Moses from the fire, when the bush burned but was not consumed,[21] in order to show forth its nature and make known its power. It was a light that in a pillar of fire guided Israel and tamed the desert.[22] It was a light that carried off Elijah in the chariot of fire[23] and did not burn up the one being carried. It was a light that flashed like lightning around the shepherds,[24] when the timeless light was mingled with what is in time. It was a light of the star hastening to Bethlehem, among other reasons to guide the magi[25] and to escort the light above us that has come to be with us. It was a light, the divinity that showed itself upon the mountain to the disciples,[26] a little too strong for their eyesight. It was a light, the vision that flashed like lightning around

[15]Gen 1.2–5.
[16]Gen 1.14–17.
[17]Gen 2.16–17.
[18]Ps 119.105.
[19]Prov 6.23.
[20]Exod 34.29–30, 35.
[21]Exod 3.2.
[22]Exod 13.21.
[23]2 Kgs 2.11.
[24]Luke 2.9.
[25]Matt 2.9.
[26]Matt 17.2, Mark 9.3, Luke 9.29.

Paul and wounded his eyesight, healing the darkness of his soul.[27]
It is a light, the radiance hereafter for those who have been purified
here, when the just will shine forth like the sun,[28] when they will be
gods and kings[29] and God will stand in their midst, determining
and distinguishing the ranks of the blessedness there. A light in the
proper sense, beyond these, is the light of baptism, the subject of
our present discourse, which encompasses a great and wondrous
mystery of our salvation.

7   For since not to sin at all belongs to God and to the first and
uncompounded nature—for simplicity is peaceable and without
discord—I make bold to say the same of the angelic nature, or that it
is the closest to this because of its closeness to God. On the contrary,
to sin belongs to humanity and the compound nature here below,
for composition is the source of discord. The Master considered it
necessary not to leave that which he himself molded[30] without help,
nor to overlook the danger of its separation from him. But as he
created what did not exist, so he remolded what did exist, through
a molding more divine than the first and more exalted, For those
beginning life this is a seal, but for those of a more mature age it is a
grace and a restoration of the image[31] wounded by evil. The grace is
given that we might not become worse through despair and ever be
borne downward toward what is bad, falling completely outside the
good and virtue, nor, having fallen into an abyss of evil, as it is said,[32]
be disdainful. Rather, it is given so that like those traveling on a long
road and resting from their labors at an inn, we will complete the
remainder of our journey renewed and with eagerness. This is the
grace and power of baptism, not a flood inundating the world as of

27 Acts 9.3–9, 18.
28 Wis 3.7, LXX.
29 Ps 81.1, 6, LXX.
30 Gen 2.7.
31 Gen 1.26–27.
32 Prov 18.3.

old, but the purification of each from sin and their complete cleansing from the heaps and defilements introduced by evil.

8 Since we are twofold, I mean composed of soul and body, and our nature is visible yet also invisible, the purification is also twofold, through water, I say, and Spirit.[33] The one is received in a way that can be seen, and is bodily, as the other joins with it incorporeally and in a way that cannot be seen. And the one is symbolic while the other is true and purifies the depths. It brings assistance to the first birth, making new instead of old and deiform instead of what we now are, recasting without fire and re-creating without shattering. For if one must say it briefly, the power of baptism is to be understood as a covenant with God for a second life and a purer lifestyle. And what is most to be feared, against which we each must guard our own soul with all watchfulness, is that we might show this agreement to be a lie. For if God is taken as a mediator to confirm agreements between human beings, how great is the danger if we are found to be transgressors of the covenant made with God himself and are thus accountable to the truth not only for other sins but also for that lie? And this when there is no second rebirth,[34] no refashioning, and no restoration to the original state, even if we should seek this to the utmost with many groans and tears, from which with difficulty comes scarring over of the wounds, according to my principles and rule of conduct. For this will come and we believe it; but if we could even wipe away the scars, I would be well pleased, since I myself also need lovingkindness. However, it is better not to need a second purification but to stop at the first, which I know to be common to all, free from toil and equally honorable for slaves, masters, poor, rich, lowly, exalted, nobles, commoners, debtors, those without debt, as the air is breathed and light shines and seasons change, the spectacle of creation. It is a great delight common to all of us, and an equal share in the faith.

[33]John 3.5.
[34]John 3.3–4. Gregory wrote before the sacrament of confession took its present form and became known as a second baptism.

9 For it is dreadful, instead of a remedy free from labor, to use the more laborious one, and throwing away the opportune grace of compassion, to owe a debt of punishment and undergo correction proportionate to sin. For how many tears must we offer to equal the fount of baptism? And who will guarantee that death will wait for the cure, and that the tribunal will not receive us still indebted and needing the fire of the hereafter? You, the good and merciful farmer, may perchance implore the Master still to spare the fig tree[35] and not yet cut it down when accusing it of unfruitfulness, but consent to put dung around it, that is tears, groans, invocations, sleeping on the ground, vigils, wasting away of soul and body, correction through public confession and a more dishonorable way of life. Yet it is unclear whether the Master will spare the fig tree, since it occupies the place uselessly while another is in need of lovingkindness and becomes worse because of the longsuffering toward the first one. So let us be buried with Christ through baptism,[36] that we may also rise with him.[37] Let us descend with him, that we may also be exalted with him. Let us ascend with him, that we may also be glorified with him.[38]

10 If after baptism the persecutor and tempter of the light attacks you—and he will attack you, for he even attacked the Word, my God, through his bodily covering, the hidden light through that which appeared—you have a way to conquer. Do not fear the struggle. Defend yourself with the water, defend yourself with the Spirit, in which all the fiery darts of the Evil One are extinguished.[39] He is a Spirit, but he melts mountains.[40] It is water, but it extinguishes fire. If [the enemy] attacks you in your need—for he also dared to do this

[35]Luke 13.6–9.
[36]Rom 6.4, Col 2.12.
[37]Eph 2.6.
[38]Rom 8.17.
[39]Eph 6.16.
[40]Ps 97.5.

to Christ—and seeks to have stones become bread[41] while bringing on hunger, do not be ignorant of his thoughts. Teach what he has not learned, oppose him with the word of life, which is the bread sent down from heaven that gives life to the world.[42] If he plots against you with vainglory—for he also did this to Christ, leading him to the pinnacle of the temple and saying, "Throw yourself down,"[43] to manifest his divinity—do not be brought down through elevation. If he takes you by this, he will not stop at this. He is insatiable, he attacks everything. He beguiles with what is useful, but it ends in wickedness. This is his way of fighting. But also, as a thief, he is acquainted with Scripture. There he says "it is written" regarding the bread;[44] here he says "it is written" regarding the angels. "For it is written," he says, "he shall command his angels concerning you, and they will lift you in their hands."[45] O deceptive advocate of evil, how could you suppress what follows? For I understand this completely, though you are silent, because I will tread upon you, the asp and the basilisk, and I will walk upon serpents and scorpions,[46] protected, as with walls, by the Trinity. If he would overthrow you with greed, giving a glimpse of all the kingdoms, as if they belonged to him,[47] in one moment and one glance, demanding worship, despise him as poor. Say, confident in the seal of baptism, "I am also myself an image of God. I have not yet fallen, like you, from the glory on high through seeking elevation. I have put on Christ,[48] I have been transformed into Christ by baptism. You should worship me." He will depart,[49] I know clearly, defeated and shamed by this; as from Christ the first light, so he will depart from those illumined by him. Such are the

[41]Matt 4.3.
[42]John 6.33.
[43]Matt 4.6.
[44]Matt 4.3–4, Luke 4.3–4.
[45]Ps 91.11–12, Matt 4.6, Luke 4.10–11.
[46]Ps 90.13, LXX.
[47]Matt 4.8–9, Luke 4.5–8.
[48]Gal 3.27.
[49]Matt 4.11, Luke 4.13.

gifts of the bath to those who have perceived it. Such is the abundant feast it provides to those who hunger well.

11   Let us be baptized, then, that we may be victorious. Let us participate in the purifying waters, which cleanse more than hyssop,[50] and purify more than blood prescribed by the Law. They are more holy that the ashes of a heifer that sprinkles the partakers[51] and bring a temporary cleansing of the body[52] but not a complete removal of sin. For why did they need purification having once been purified? Let us be baptized today so that we are not forced into it tomorrow, let us not postpone the benefit, as if it were an injury, or wait to become more evil, that we may be forgiven more, or become marketers and traders of Christ, or become vessels laden with more than we can carry, lest we be sunk,[53] the ship and the whole crew, and be shipwrecked in regard to the gift, and instead of having great hope lose everything. While you are still in possession of your reason, run to the gift, while you are not yet sick in body and in mind, and you do not appear so to those with you, though you are of sound mind, while your good does not depend on others, but you are yourself in control of it. Run while your tongue is not stammering or parched or unable—to say no more—to speak the words of your initiation; while you can become a believer, not conjecturally, but confessedly, as one not pitied but deemed happy; while the gift is clear to you, and not doubtful, and the grace touches you to the depth instead of washing your body for burial, while no tears are around you announcing your departure, nor are they perhaps held back for your sake, while your wife and children delay your journey and search for your dying words. Run to baptism while the physician is not powerless to help you, giving you hours of which he is not master, and weighing your

---

[50]Exod 12.22, Num 19.6, Ps 51.7, Heb 9.19.
[51]Num 19.2–4, 9.
[52]Heb 9.13, 10.4.
[53]Here the same Greek word can mean either "to be baptized" or "to be sunk." Gregory is clearly playing with this ambiguity.

salvation in the balance by a nod, and lecturing about the illness after your death, or increasing his charges by withdrawals, or hinting at despair. Run while there is no conflict between the baptizer and the businessman, the one striving for a way to provide supplies for the journey, the other for a way to be inscribed as an heir, when time does not allow for both.

12 Why do you await fever as a benefactor but not God? Why do you look to the occasion but not to reason? Why to a plotting friend and not to a saving desire? Why not by your own power but by force? Why not with freedom but with constraint? Why must you learn from another of your departure instead of understanding it as already present? Why do you search for medicines that are no help? Or the sweat decisive for recovery, which could equally bring near your departure? Heal yourself before the extremity, have mercy on yourself, for you are the true healer of your sickness. Apply to yourself the really saving medicine. While you sail with the fair winds, fear shipwreck, and you will have less risk of shipwreck if you use the fear as a helper. Let the gift bring feasting, not mourning. Let the talent be cultivated, not buried in the ground.[54] Let there be some time between the gift and the dissolution, that not only may the record of evils be wiped out, but better things may also be written, that you may not have only the gift but also the reward, that you may not only flee the fire but also inherit the glory, which is granted to those who cultivate the gift. For to those of small soul it is a great thing to flee torment, but those of great soul seek also to obtain a reward.

13 For I know three ranks among the saved: the slaves, the hired servants and the sons. If you are a slave, fear the blows; if a hired servant, look only to receive your pay. But if you are above these and are a son, respect God as a Father. Work to do good, for it is good to obey your Father, even if this will bring nothing for you. This itself

[54]Matt 25.14–30.

is a reward, to please your Father. Let us show that we do not despise it. How absurd it is to grasp at riches but throw away health, and to cleanse the body first but skimp on the cleansing of the soul, and to seek freedom from the slavery here below and not aim for the freedom above, and put all one's zeal into how to be housed or clothed magnificently while not caring how oneself could be of the greatest value, and be eager to do good to others but not want the same for oneself. And if the good had been on sale to you, you would have spared no expense, yet if the lovingkindness lies before you, you despise the beneficence as readily available. Every moment is right for your washing, since any time could bring your death. With Paul, that great voice, I cry out to you, "Behold, now is the acceptable time, behold now is the day of salvation."[55] "Now" specifies not one time but every time. And again, "Get up, sleeper, and rise from the dead, and Christ will shine upon you,"[56] dissolving the night of sin, since "in the night hope is wicked,"[57] according to Isaiah, "and to be taken in early morning is more advantageous."[58]

14 Sow when it is the right time, and gather and open your barns when it is time for this, and plant in season, and cut the cluster of grapes when it is ripe. Put out to sea with confidence in spring, and haul your ship ashore again when winter begins and the sea is fierce. And let there be for you a time of war and of peace, of marriage and of not marrying, of friendship and of separation, if this is necessary, and in short a time for everything, if Solomon's word is to be believed.[59] And it is to be believed, for indeed the advice is useful. But always work at your salvation and let every time be earmarked for your baptism. If you always bypass today and look forward to tomorrow, by these delays little by little you will be cheated by the Evil One, as is his way: "Give the present to me, the future to God;

[55]2 Cor 6.2.
[56]Eph 5.14.
[57]Isa 28.19, LXX.
[58]Reference uncertain.
[59]Eccl 3.1–8.

your youth to me, your old age to God; pleasures to me, uselessness to him." What great danger surrounds you, what unexpected mishaps! War has liquidated you, or an earthquake overwhelmed you, or the sea engulfed you, or a wild beast seized you, or a disease killed you, or a crumb going down the wrong way, the smallest thing—for what is easier than for a human being to die, though you are proud of the divine image?—or drinking was excessive, or a wind knocked you down, or a horse ran away with its rider, or a drug was prepared in a plot against you, or maybe it turned out to harm you instead of healing, or a judge was inhuman, or an executioner inexorable, or whatever causes a departure that is very quick and beyond help.

15 Yet if you prepare yourself beforehand by the seal, and make the future secure by the most beautiful and solid of helps, being signed in both soul and body by the chrism and the Spirit, as Israel was of old by the anointing of blood at night that protected their firstborn,[60] what can befall you and what has been worked out for you? Listen to Proverbs. "If you sit," it says, "you will be without fear; and if you lie down, you will sleep contentedly."[61] And hear the good news from David. "You will not fear the terror by night, nor the mishap or demon of midday."[62] This, also while you live, will bring you the greatest security. For a marked sheep is not easily plotted against, but an unmarked one is easily taken by thieves. And when you depart it will be a propitious funeral gift, more brilliant than a robe, more valuable than gold, more magnificent than a tomb, more reverent than fruitless libations, more timely than ripe firstfruits, which the dead give to the dead,[63] making a law out of a custom. Let everything be lost to you, let everything be seized, wealth, property, thrones, splendors, whatever makes the rounds here below; yet you will end your life in security without being deprived of the helps given you from God for salvation.

[60]Exod 12.21–24.
[61]Prov 3.24, LXX.
[62]Ps 90.5–6, LXX.
[63]Matt 8.22.

16 Yet do you fear ruining the gift, and because of this postpone the purification, since you do not have a second chance? But why? Do you fear being endangered at a time of persecution and being deprived of the greatest good you have, Christ? So is it because of this that you avoid becoming a Christian? Forget it! The fear does not belong to one of sound mind, the thought is that of one deranged. O impious piety, if one must speak thus. O trick of the Evil One! He is truly darkness and masquerades as light.[64] When he has no strength when making war openly, he plots secretly and gives advice as if it were useful, though it is wicked, in case somehow at any rate he may prove stronger, and we may have nowhere to escape from his plotting. So this is clearly what he is contriving here. Since he cannot persuade you to despise baptism openly, he does damage to you through counterfeit security, that because of your fear you may suffer unawares that which you fear; and having dreaded to ruin the gift, might through this dread itself be deprived of the gift. So then he is like this, and he will never cease from his own duplicity, as long as he sees us hastening to heaven, from where he has himself fallen.[65] But you, O person of God,[66] know the plot of the adversary. For the battle is against one who possesses, and it concerns the greatest matters. Do not take the enemy as an adviser; do not despise to become and to be called "faithful." As long as you are a catechumen, you are on the front porch of piety. You must come inside, cross the court, observe the Holy Things, look into the Holy of Holies, be with the Trinity. Great are the things for which you fight; great also for you must be the security. Defend yourself with the shield of faith.[67] He fears you since you fight armed, and because of this he would strip you of the grace, in order to conquer you more easily as one unarmed and unprotected. He attacks all ages, all modes of life. Let him be driven off by all!

[64]2 Cor 11.14.
[65]Luke 10.18.
[66]1 Tim 6.11.
[67]Eph 6.16.

17   Are you young? Stand against the passions with this alliance. Be counted in the ranks of God's army, be most valiant against Goliath,[68] take thousands or tens of thousands.[69] Enjoy the prime of your life in this way, but do not let your youth be withered, killed by immaturity of faith. Are you old and near the foreordained necessity? Respect your gray hair, give it the prudence owed to it in compensation for the weakness you now have; help your few remaining days, entrust the purification to your old age. Why fear the things of youth in the depth of age and at your last breath? Or are you waiting to be washed until you are dead, and not so much pitied as abhorred? Or do you desire the last remains of pleasure, as you are in the last remnant of life? It is shameful when past the prime of life not to be past the prime of licentiousness, but either to experience this or appear to do so by delaying your purification. Do you have a small child? Let evil not seize this time, let him be sanctified from babyhood, let him be consecrated by the Spirit from when his nails grow. Have you been afraid of the seal because of the weakness of nature? You are a mother of small soul and weak faith. Yet Anna, even before Samuel was born, promised him to God,[70] and when he was born immediately consecrated him[71] and brought him up with the priestly vestment,[72] not fearing human concerns but believing in God. You do not need amulets and incantations, with which the Evil One enters in, stealing reverence from God for himself, among the more light-minded. Give your child the Trinity, the great and beautiful safeguard.

18   What else? Do you practice virginity? Be marked with the seal of purification; make this the companion of your life, your associate. Let it bring into order for you life and reason, all your limbs, all movements, all perceptions. Honor it, that it may adorn you, that it

[68]1 Sam 17.50.
[69]1 Sam 18.7.
[70]1 Sam 1.11.
[71]1 Sam 1.28.
[72]1 Sam 2.18–19.

may give to your head a crown of graces, and may shield you with a crown of delights.[73] Have you been bound in marriage? Be bound by the seal also; let this live with you as a guard of your chastity. Do you not consider it to be more secure than any number of eunuchs and doorkeepers? Are you not yet yoked to another in the flesh? Do not fear the complete initiation. You are pure also after marriage. The risk is mine, I will join you together. I will escort the bride. It does not follow that since virginity is more honorable, marriage is without honor. I will imitate Christ, the pure bridal escort and bridegroom,[74] who also worked a miracle at a wedding and honored wedlock by his presence.[75] Only let the marriage be pure and unmixed with filthy desires. I ask only one thing, receive the security along with the gift, and give to the gift continence in due season when the appointed time for prayer and what is more valuable than business comes. Do this by common agreement and consent.[76] For we do not establish laws, but we give advice,[77] and we would like to receive something of yours for your benefit and for the sake of the common security of both of you. To summarize, there is no way of life or occupation in which baptism is not advantageous. You who are in authority, accept it as a bridle; you who are in slavery, as equality of honor; you who are discouraged, as encouragement; you who are cheerful, as training; you who are poor, as wealth that cannot be stolen; you who are affluent, as good management of what you possess. Do not play subtle tricks or connive cunningly against your own salvation. For even if we mislead others, we cannot do it to ourselves. For to play games with oneself is very dangerous and stupid.

19 But are you in the midst of the whirl and stained by public affairs, and do you fear that you may waste the divine lovingkindness? My word to you is simple. If you can, flee even the public

---

[73]Prov 4.9.
[74]Eph 5.23–27, 2 Cor 11.2, John 3.29.
[75]John 2.1–11.
[76]1 Cor 7.5.
[77]1 Cor 7.6.

square in company with good people, put on yourself the wings of an eagle, or of a dove, to speak more properly. For what indeed have you to do with Caesar or the things of Caesar?[78] Flee until you rest where there is no sin, nor darkening, nor serpent biting by the road to hinder your steps in accord with God. Snatch your own soul from the world. Flee Sodom, flee the fire. Travel without looking back, lest you be petrified into a rock of salt.[79] Be saved on the mountain,[80] lest you be taken with the others. Yet if you are already constrained and bound by the bonds of necessity, speak thus with yourself, or rather, I myself will speak with you. It is indeed better to attain the good and guard the purification, but if both are not possible, it is better to be stained a little on some occasion by your public affairs than to lose the grace altogether, as indeed, in my view, it is better to receive some criticism from father or master than to be thrown out, and better to shine a little than to be entirely darkened. And as it is a characteristic of the prudent to choose among goods the greatest and most perfect, so also among evils to choose the least and lightest. For this reason do not fear the purification too much. For always to judge success in accord with people's occupations is a characteristic of our just and compassionate judge. And for one in the midst of various things to succeed a little is often better than for one free of such business not to succeed completely, just as, in my view, it is more astonishing to step forward a little in shackles than to run when carrying no load, and to be spattered a little when walking through mud than to be clean on a clean road. As proof of what I have said, consider Rahab the prostitute, who was justified by one thing alone, hospitality,[81] though not commended for other things, and the tax collector, who was exalted by one thing, humility,[82] but received no testimonial for anything else, that you may learn not to despair easily of yourself.

[78]Matt 22.21, Mark 12.17, Luke 20.25.
[79]Gen 19.17, 24–26.
[80]Gen 19.17.
[81]Josh 2.1–21, 6.17, 22–23.
[82]Luke 18.13–14.

20   But what more is there for me, some say, if I am restrained beforehand by baptism and have excluded myself by my haste from the delight of living, when I could give myself to pleasure and then attain the grace? For those who labored first in the vineyard have nothing more, since the wage given is equal even for those who were last.[83] You have saved me some trouble, whoever you are that say this, in speaking forth with difficulty the unspoken reason for the delay. And though not praising your misconduct, I praise your disclosure. But come and hear the explanation of the parable, so as not to be harmed through inexperience by what is written. First, the text here is not about baptism but about those believing and entering into the good vineyard, the church, at different times. For from the day and hour in which each believed, from that time one is also required to work. Therefore if indeed by the measure of toil those who entered first offered more, they did not do so by the measure of good will. And perhaps because of this more is even owed to those who were last, though indeed the statement is somehow paradoxical. For they entered later because they were also called later to the work of the vineyard. And let us consider how much they differed from the others. The first did not believe or enter prior to an agreement with them about wages; the last undertook the work without an agreement, which is a sign of greater faith. And the first were found to be of an envious and murmuring nature, but the last were not accused of any such thing. And to the first wages were given, even if they were wicked, but to the last, grace. So also the first, accused of stupidity, were rightly deprived of something greater. Let us understand what would have been given to them if they had come late. Clearly, an equal wage. How can they question the one giving the work on account of the inequality of the equality? All these things take away from the favor owed to the sweat of the first, even if they toiled earlier. What results from this? The equal distribution is just, since the good will is counted instead of the labor.

[83]Matt 20.1ff.

21   Yet even if the parable depicts the power of the washing according to your interpretation, what prevents you who have entered first and borne the heat from avoiding envy to the end, thinking that because of this lovingkindness you may have more, and receive the recompense as something owed you, not as a favor? Further, the workers who received it entered there, not those who missed the vineyard, which is an experience you risk. So if it were clear that you would obtain the gift, though you have such an attitude and maliciously withhold some of the work, you could be pardoned for appealing to such arguments and desiring to gain something unjustly from the Master's lovingkindness. Yet I could say that the increased toil itself is a greater recompense to one who does not have entirely the mind of a shopkeeper. But if you risk missing the vineyard altogether because of this bargaining and losing the capital while collecting pittances here and there, come, be persuaded by my words. Let go of such misinterpretations and objections, and come to the gift without arguing, lest you be snatched away beforehand without realizing your hopes and deceive yourself unawares by such reasonings.

22   But then, you say, does the Deity not love humankind? For knowing our thoughts, does he not approve our desire and make the intention to be baptized take the place of baptism? What you say is like a riddle. It is as if God because of love considered the unillumined to be illumined, or as if one is within the kingdom of heaven by being eager to obtain it, without doing the deeds of the kingdom. But as for me, I make bold to say what I think about these matters, and my understanding is that others who have sense will also agree. Of those who obtain the gift, some were entirely strangers to God and to salvation, passing completely through every form of evil, and zealous to be evil. Some were in some way half bad and were in the middle between virtue and evil. They practiced evil but did not approve of what they practiced, just as those who have a fever disapprove of their illness. Others even before the initiation were praiseworthy, since either by nature or through zeal they purified themselves before baptism. And after their initiation they have been shown as better and more secure, either in attaining the good or in preserving it. Among these, those who yield to some evil are better than those who are entirely wicked; and those who are more zealous and cultivate themselves before baptism are better than those who yield in a small matter, for they have something more, their work. For the bath does not destroy good actions as it wipes out sins. And better than these are those who both cultivate the grace and polish themselves to become as beautiful as possible.

23 So also among those who fail to obtain baptism, some are entirely animal or bestial, depending whether they are stupid or wicked. They, along with their other vices, in my view, do not respect the grace very much, though it truly is grace. If it is given they accept it gladly, but if it is not given they despise it. Others know and honor the gift, but they put it off, either through heedlessness or through greed. Others do not have the power to receive it, either through infancy, perhaps, or some absolutely involuntary circumstance, because of which even if they desire it they cannot obtain the grace. As, then, among the former group we found the greatest differences, so too among these. Those who despise it completely are worse than those who are greedy or heedless, and they are worse than those who because of ignorance or constraint lose the gift. For constraint is nothing other than involuntary error. And I believe the first will also pay a penalty, both for their wickedness and also for despising the bath. The second will pay, but less, since they brought about their failure to attain it through stupidity rather than evil. The others will neither be glorified nor punished by the just judge,[84] since they did not receive the seal yet were not wicked, but suffered rather than did the damage. For not everyone who does not deserve punishment is at the same time honored, just as not everyone who is not honored

[84] 2 Tim 4.8.

is at the same time also punished. And I look at it also as follows. If you judge as a murderer one who only wanted to commit a murder but did no murder, then you can consider baptized one who wanted baptism without being baptized. If I cannot accept the one, how can I accept the other? If you like, look at it this way. If for you the desire has the same power as actual baptism, and hence you consider that you will have life without baptism, the enjoyment of glory is entirely superfluous. For if you argue in this way about glory, the desire for glory will be enough for you instead of glory. And what is it to you not to attain it, since you have the aspiration?

24   Therefore, after you have heard these words, "Come to him and be illumined and your faces will not be ashamed"[85] through failing to obtain the grace. And receive the illumination while there is time, that darkness may not pursue and overtake you,[86] separating you from the illumination. "Night is coming, when nobody is able to work,"[87] after the departure from here. The one text is the voice of David, the other of the true Light that illumines every human being coming into the world.[88] Consider also that Solomon sharply reproaches you who are too idle and sluggish, saying, "How long will you lie down, lazy one?" and, "When will you rise from sleep?"[89] You allege this or that and "make excuses in sins."[90] "I am waiting for Theophany, Pascha would be more valuable for me, I will wait for Pentecost; it is better to be illumined with Christ, or to rise with Christ on the day of resurrection, or to honor the manifestation of the Spirit." Then what? The end will come suddenly on a day that you do not expect and at an hour that you do not know.[91] Then you will have with you, as a bad fellow traveler, a poverty of grace, and you

---

[85]Ps 34.5.
[86]John 12.35.
[87]John 9.4.
[88]John 1.9.
[89]Prov 6.9.
[90]Ps 140.4, LXX.
[91]Luke 12.19–20.

will starve amid such a great wealth of goodness. You need to reap the opposite fruit in the opposite way, with the harvest of diligence and the spring of refreshment, like the deer parched with thirst rushing eagerly toward the springs[92] and quenching the fatigue of its running with water, but not like what Ishmael suffered, being dried up by lack of water,[93] or, as in the myth, being punished by thirst in the middle of a spring.[94] It is terrible to let the market day pass and then seek to do business. It is terrible to pass by the manna and then long for food. It is terrible to decide too late and then to perceive the damage, when there is no remedy for the damage, after the departure from here and the cruel closure of the acts of each person's life, and the punishment of sinners, and the splendor of those who have been purified. For this reason, do not delay coming to grace, but hurry, lest the thief take it before you, lest the adulterer pass by you, lest the greedy have a larger share, lest the murderer seize the good before you, or the tax collector, or the prostitute,[95] or any who with violence seize the kingdom.[96] For it willingly suffers violence and is tyrannized through goodness.

25 Go slowly toward evildoing, my friend, and quickly toward salvation, if you are persuaded by me, for these are equal evils, readiness for the worse and delay of the better. If you are invited to a wild party, do not hasten; if you are invited to apostasy, turn away; if a wicked gang says to you, "Come with us, share in bloodshed, and let us unjustly bury in the earth a just man,"[97] do not lend an ear. For you

[92]Ps 42.1.

[93]Gen 21.15–19.

[94]This refers to the myth of Tantalus, who is punished after death for cutting up, cooking and serving his son at a feast. In the underworld he is immersed in water up to his neck while tree branches bearing luscious fruit hang above him. When he bends to drink the water it drains away, and when he reaches to pluck the fruit it moves beyond his reach. Hence the word "tantalize." See also Oration 39.5 and my first note on the paragraph.

[95]Matt 21.31.

[96]Matt 11.12.

[97]Prov 1.11.

will gain two very great advantages: you will make known to them their sin and remove yourself from their wicked companionship. But if the great David says to you, "Come, let us rejoice in the Lord,"[98] and if another prophet says, "Come, let us go up to the mountain of the Lord,"[99] and if the Savior himself says, "Come to me, all who labor and are heavy laden, and I will give you rest,"[100] or "Rise, let us go from here,"[101] shining brightly, brighter than snow, than curdled milk, more radiant than a sapphire stone,[102] let us not resist, let us not be slow. Let us become Peter and John; as they hastened to the tomb and the resurrection,[103] so let us hasten to the bath, running together, racing against each other, struggling to receive the blessing first. And do not say, "Go away, come back and I will be baptized tomorrow," though you could receive the blessing today. "Let my mother be with me, let my father be with me, my brothers and sisters, wife, children, friends, all whom I value, and then I will be saved; but now is not yet the time for me to be made radiant." For there is a risk that you will receive as sharers in mourning those you hoped would be sharers in joy. If they are present, be pleased, but if they are absent, do not wait. It is shameful to say, "Where is the offering I will make at my illumination? And where is the baptismal robe in which I will be made radiant? And where are the means to greet my baptizers, that through this I may be esteemed?" For all these things, as you see it, are necessary, and apart from this the grace will be diminished. Do not quibble about great things, do not allow yourself such ignoble thoughts. The mystery is greater than visible things. Offer yourself, clothe yourself with Christ,[104] feed me by your way of life; thus I rejoice to be entertained, and thus also does God, who gives the greatest gifts. To God, nothing is great that a poor person

[98]Ps 94.1.
[99]Mic 4.2.
[100]Matt 11.28.
[101]John 14.31.
[102]Lam 4.7.
[103]John 20.3–4.
[104]Rom 13.14, Gal 3.27.

cannot give, lest even here the poor should be rejected; for they do not have the means to compete with the rich. In other respects there is a difference between the rich and the poor, but here the more eager is the richer.

26   Let nothing stop you from moving forward, let nothing hold back your eagerness. While your desire is vehement, receive what you desire. While the iron is hot, harden it in the cold water, lest something come in between and cut off the desire. I am Philip; become Candace's eunuch. May you also say, "Here is water. What prevents my being baptized?"[105] Seize the opportunity, rejoice greatly in the blessing. And having spoken, be baptized; and having been baptized, be saved. Even if you are an Ethiopian in your body, be whitened in your soul. Attain salvation; nothing is more exalted or honorable than this to sensible people. Do not say, "Let a bishop baptize me, and let him be a metropolitan bishop, or bishop of Jerusalem"—for grace is not from a place but from the Spirit—"and let him be nobly born, for it would be dreadful if my nobility were insulted by my baptizer," or, "Let a priest do it, but let him be celibate and one of the ascetics and angelic in his way of life, for it would be dreadful if I were made dirty at the time of my purification." Do not seek trustworthiness in the preacher or in the baptizer. Another is his judge, and he examines things that are not manifest, since a human being will see the face, but God will see the heart.[106] But all are trustworthy for your purification, only let it be someone among those approved and not openly condemned or a stranger to the Church. Do not judge your judges, you who need healing. Do not judge the rank of those who purify you, and do not make distinctions regarding those who give you birth. One may be greater or another more lowly, but all are more exalted than you. Look at it this way. Though one is gold and one is iron, two rings are both truly engraved with the same imperial image, then are pressed

[105] Acts 8.36.
[106] 1 Sam 16.7.

into wax. What will be the difference between the seal of one and the seal of the other? Nothing. Recognize the ring's material from the wax, if you are so very wise, and say which is the impression of the iron, and which is of the gold, and how there is only one; for there is a difference in the material, not in the imprint. Let it be thus to you in regard to every baptizer. One may excel in his way of life, but the power of baptism is equal. And let every initiator be alike to you who has been formed by the same faith.

27 Do not disdain to be baptized with a poor person if you are rich, with one lowly born if you are noble, with one up to now a slave if you are a master. You are not yet humbling yourself as much as Christ, into whom you are baptized today, who for your sake even accepted "the form of a slave."[107] From the day you are transformed, all the old imprints have withdrawn; Christ has placed himself upon all as a single form. Do not disdain to confess your sin, knowing how John baptized,[108] that you may flee the coming shame through present shame—since shame is also part of the punishment to come—and show that you have in reality hated your sin, making an example of it and triumphing over it as worthy of contempt. Do not spit upon the medicine of exorcism or refuse it because of its length. This too is a touchstone of your sincerity regarding the gift. Do you labor as much as "the queen of the Ethiopians, who rose and came from the ends of the earth to see the wisdom of Solomon? And behold, a greater Solomon is here,"[109] according to those who reason maturely. Do not draw back from either the length of the road, or the distance of the sea, or fire, if indeed it lies before you, or any other obstacle, either small or great, so as to attain the grace. But if with neither labor nor trouble you can attain what you desire, how silly to delay the gift. "You who thirst," Scripture says, "come to the water"—Isaiah exhorts you—"and as many as have no money,

[107]Phil 2.7.
[108]Matt 3.6, Mark 1.5.
[109]Matt 12.42, 1 Kgs 10.1–3.

come, buy, and drink wine," without price.[110] O swiftness of love
for humankind! O ease of reconciliation! The blessing is on sale to
you for your will alone; God accepts the yearning itself as a high
price. He thirsts to be thirsted for, he gives a drink to those wishing
to drink, he is benefited by being asked for benefit. The great gift is
at hand; he gives with more pleasure than others take in receiving.
Only let us not be condemned for pettiness in asking for small things
unworthy of the giver. Blessed is one of whom Christ asks a drink,
like that Samaritan woman, and to whom he gives "a fountain of
water springing up to eternal life."[111] "Blessed is one who sows on
every water"[112] and on every soul, which tomorrow is plowed and
watered, though today it is trodden by the ox and the donkey, since
it is dry and waterless and pressed down by lack of reason. Blessed is
one who, though a torrent of rushes, gives drink from the house of
the Lord,[113] and becomes a grain bearer instead of a rush-bearer and
cultivates food that is fit for human beings, not harsh and useless.
For the sake of this it is necessary to bring all eagerness so as not to
fail in obtaining the grace common to all.

28 So be it, some will say, for those seeking baptism. But what
would you say about those who are still infants and perceive neither
the damage nor the grace? Should we baptize them also? Absolutely,
if indeed there is some immediate danger. For it is better to be sanctified without perceiving it than to depart unsealed and uninitiated.
And for us the reason for this is the circumcision on the eighth day,
which is a kind of type of the seal and is conferred on those who
still lack reason,[114] and likewise the anointing of the doorposts
which guarded the firstborn by means of inert[115] things.[116] But as

[110]Isa 55.1.
[111]John 4.7–14.
[112]Isa 32.20.
[113]Joel 3.18, LXX.
[114]Gen 17.12.
[115]In Greek, "without perceiving it" and "inert" are forms of the same word.
[116]Exod 12.22–23, 29.

for the rest I give my recommendation to wait for the third year, or a little more or a little less, when they can also hear something of the mystery and respond, so even if they do not understand completely, at any rate they are imprinted. And then sanctify them in both soul and body by the great mystery of initiation. For indeed the situation is as follows. They begin to be responsible for their lives at the time when their reason is matured and they learn the mystery, for because of their age the sins due to ignorance are not their responsibility. And it is more useful in every respect to be fortified by the bath because the sudden assaults of danger that befall us are beyond help.

29   But Christ, some will say, is baptized at age thirty,[117] and that although he is God, and you exhort me to hasten baptism? In saying he is God you have resolved the question. For he who was purification itself did not need purification but is purified for you, as indeed he also bears flesh though he is without flesh. And there was no danger for him in postponing baptism, for he himself was indeed the director of his own passion, as also of his birth. But for you the danger is far from small, if you depart born to corruption alone and not clothed in incorruption.[118] And I consider that for him it was necessary to be baptized on the right occasion, but your case is not the same. For he was manifested when he became thirty years of age, not before, that he might not appear ostentatious—for this is a weakness of the vulgar—and since to this age belong a perfectly tested virtue and an opportunity to teach. And because he had to undergo the passion for the world's salvation, all things that pertain to the passion had to converge toward the passion: the manifestation, the baptism, the testimony from above, the proclamation, the crowd coming together, the miracles. And these events became like one body, not dispersed or broken apart by intervals of time. For from the baptism and the proclamation came the earthquake of people

[117]Luke 3.23.
[118]1 Cor 15.50.

coming together[119]—for thus Scripture names that occasion—and from the crowd came the showing forth of signs and the miracles that lead to the gospel. And from this came the envy, and from this the hatred; and from the hatred the plot and the betrayal, and from this the cross and events by which we have been saved. For Christ, this indeed is the case, as far as we can perceive it. Perhaps someone may also find another explanation more mysterious than this.

30   But as for you, what requires you, in following an example that is above you, to decide badly? For indeed many other events of that time are portrayed in biblical narrative as different from the way things happen today, and they do not correspond in regard to time. For instance, he fasted a little before the temptation,[120] we do before Pascha; the fasts are one, but the distance between the times of each is not small. For he uses the fast to arm himself against the temptations, while it enables our dying with Christ and is a pre-festal purification. And he fasts for forty days, for he is God, while we measure it according to our ability, though indeed zeal also tempts some to shoot beyond their ability. Again, he initiates the disciples into the mystery of Pascha in the upper room,[121] and after a meal, and one day before the passion; we do this in houses of prayer, and before a meal, and after the resurrection. He rises on the third day, but we will rise after many years. And our conduct has neither been torn away from his nor bound to it chronologically, but his conduct has been handed down to the extent of being a model for ours while avoiding a complete likeness. Why, then, is it any wonder that he has taken on baptism for us, yet with a difference in time? It seems to me that through reaching for something great and wondrous you arm yourself against your own salvation.

[119]Matt 21.10.
[120]Matt 4.2, Luke 4.2.
[121]Mark. 14.15ff, Luke 22.11ff.

31   If, then, you are persuaded by me, let all such arguments depart. And you will jump at the blessing and struggle on two fronts, first to purify yourselves before baptism, then to preserve the baptism, since the same difficulty is involved in obtaining blessings we do not have and in keeping those we possess. For often what zeal has received, heedlessness has utterly destroyed, and what hesitation has ruined, care has called back. There is great help for you toward the attainment of what you desire in vigils, fasts, sleeping on the ground, prayers, tears, compassion for the needy, and sharing. Let this become for you thanksgiving for what you have obtained and at the same time a safeguard. You have the benefit of baptism as a reminder of many commandments; do not pass them by. Has a poor person come to you? Remember how poor you were and how much you have been enriched. Has someone in need of bread and drink, perhaps another Lazarus, thrown himself before your gates?[122] Respect the mystical table that you have approached, the bread of which you have partaken, the cup in which you have participated, having been initiated through the sufferings of Christ. A stranger has fallen before you, homeless, a foreigner. Receive into your house through him the one who became a stranger for your sake, even among his own,[123] and dwelt in you through grace,[124] and drew you toward the dwelling place on high. Become Zaccheus,[125] who was a tax collector yesterday and today is magnanimous. Bear every fruit for the entry of Christ that you may show yourself as great, even if you are small in bodily height, nobly looking upon Christ. Does someone sick and wounded lie before you? Respect your health and the wounds from which Christ freed you.[126] "If you see someone naked, cover him,"[127] honoring your robe of incorruption. This robe is Christ, "for as many

---

[122]Luke 16.20ff.
[123]John 1.11.
[124]John 14.23.
[125]Luke 19.2–10.
[126]Isa 53.4–5.
[127]Isa 58.7.

as have been baptized into Christ have been clothed in Christ."[128]
If you receive a debtor who falls before you, tear up every contract,
whether unjust or just.[129] Remember the ten thousand talents that
Christ forgave you.[130] Do not become a cruel collector of a smaller
debt. And this from whom? From your fellow slaves, you who have
been forgiven so much by the Master. Otherwise you may have to
give a recompense to his lovingkindness, which you have not imitated, though you were given an example.

32 Let the bath not be to you for the body only, but also for the
divine image,[131] not only a washing away of sins but also a correction of character. Let it not only clean off the mud that has come
in beforehand but also purify the source. Let it not only shape you
to acquire possessions well but also to give away possessions well,
or, at the very least, to put aside what has been acquired badly. For
what use to you is the forgiveness of sin, when the damage you have
done is not repaired for the one who was wronged? Two evils belong
to you, having acquired unjustly and having held on to what was
acquired. You have received pardon for the first, but regarding the
second you are doing wrong today. For today you have what belongs
to another, and the sin is not removed but is divided by time, since
part of it was committed before baptism while part remains after
baptism. The bath brings forgiveness of past sins, not continuing
sins. And the purification must not be received deceitfully but
imprinted into you, that you may be made completely radiant, not
only colored on the surface. May the grace not just cover up your sins
but get rid of them. "Blessed are those whose iniquities are removed,"
that is by a complete purification, "and whose sins are covered," that
is those not yet purified in the depth. "Blessed is the man for whom
the Lord will not take account of sin";[132] this refers to the third kind

[128]Gal 3.27.
[129]Isa 58.6, LXX.
[130]Matt 18.25–28.
[131]Gen 1.26–27.
[132]Ps 32.1.

of sinners, whose actions are not praiseworthy, though their intention is free of guilt.

33 What, then, am I saying, and what is my argument? Yesterday you were a Canaanite[133] soul and bent[134] by sin. Today you have been made straight again by the Word. Do not bend again and incline toward the earth, as if under a yoke, weighed down by the evil one, and have a lowness hard to recall to things above. Yesterday you were dried up by the vigor of a hemorrhage,[135] for you were pouring out scarlet sin.[136] Today your vigor is renewed as you are stanched, for you touched Christ's hem[137] and the flow stopped. Guard for me the purification, lest you hemorrhage again and are not strong enough to grasp Christ, that you might steal salvation.[138] For Christ does not like to be stolen from often, though he loves humankind very much. Yesterday you were thrown onto a bed, slackened and weakened, and you had no human being to throw you into the pool when the water was agitated.[139] Today you have found a human being, the same one who is also God, or rather the God-human. You got up from your pallet, or rather picked up your pallet[140] and recorded his good deed on a monument. Do not again be thrown onto a pallet by sinning, in the evil rest of a body slackened by pleasures, but walk as you are, remembering the commandment: "Behold, you have become well; sin no more, lest something worse happen to you"[141] when you show yourself as evil after this beneficence. "Lazarus, come out."[142] Lying in a tomb, you have heard the great voice—for what voice is greater than that of the Word?—and you have come forth, as one dead not

---

[133]Matt 15.22.
[134]Luke 13.11.
[135]Matt 9.20, Mark 5.25, Luke 8.43.
[136]Isa 1.18.
[137]Matt 9.20–22, Mark 5.27–28, Luke 8.44.
[138]Mark 5.30–33.
[139]John 5.3–7.
[140]John 5.8–9.
[141]John 5.14.
[142]John 11.43.

four days[143] but many days, risen with the one who rose on the third day[144] and loosed the bonds of those in tombs. Do not again become dead and come to be with those who dwell in tombs,[145] nor bind yourself tightly with the cords[146] of your own sins. For it is unclear whether you will again rise from the tomb until the final and common resurrection, which will bring all of creation to judgment, not to be healed but to be judged and to give an account of what for good or ill it has treasured up.

34 If you were covered for a time with leprosy, that is unsightly wickedness, but you removed the evil matter and received back the image whole, show your purification to me, your priest,[147] that I may determine how much more valuable it is than that of the law. Do not become one of the nine ungrateful ones, but imitate the tenth, for even if he was a Samaritan, yet he was more prudent than the others.[148] Take precautions so that the evil does not burst forth again and your bodily disorder does not become difficult to heal. Until yesterday meanness and avarice shriveled your hand; today let it be stretched out[149] in sharing and compassion. It is a good cure for a sickly hand "to dispense, give to the poor,"[150] to draw forth what we have abundantly, until we even reach the bottom. Maybe this will even gush forth food for you—as indeed it did for the woman of Zarephath, especially if perchance you feed an Elijah[151]—so that you perceive that it is a good affluence to be needy for the sake of Christ, who for our sake became poor.[152] If you were deaf and mute,[153] let the

[143]John 11.39.
[144]Matt 20.19.
[145]Ps 68.6.
[146]John 11.44.
[147]Luke 17.14.
[148]Luke 17.15–19.
[149]Luke 6.6–10.
[150]Ps 112.9.
[151]1 Kgs 17.14–16.
[152]2 Cor 8.9.
[153]Mark 7.32.

Word sound in you, or rather keep the one who has sounded in you. Do not close your ears to the teaching and admonition of the Lord, like a snake to charms.[154] If you are blind and unillumined, "illumine your eyes lest at any time you sleep in death."[155] In the light of the Lord see light,[156] in the Spirit of God receive the radiance of the Son, the threefold and undivided light. If you receive within you the whole Word, you will gather to your own soul all of Christ's cures, by which he has cured each individually. Only do not be ignorant of the measure of grace. Only let the enemy not, as you are sleepy and careless, wickedly sow darnel.[157] Only do not, having provoked the envy of the Evil One because of your purity, again make yourself pitiable by sin. Only do not rejoice excessively and exalt yourself beyond measure over the blessing, lest you fall down by being lifted up.[158] Only labor always at your purification, "arranging ascents in your heart."[159] And having attained pardon as a free gift, preserve it by attentiveness, that while the pardon comes to you from God, the preservation may come also from you.

35 Yet how will this come about? Always remember that well-known parable and you will help yourself best and most perfectly. The unclean and gross spirit went out from you, expelled by baptism. It cannot bear its expulsion or accept being without home or hearth. It goes through waterless places that are dry without the divine stream. There it desires a place it will like, wanders seeking rest, but does not find it.[160] It encounters baptized souls, from whom the bath has washed out evil. It fears the water, drowned by the purification even as the "legion" is by the sea.[161] It turns back again toward

[154]Ps 57.5–6, LXX.
[155]Cf. Ps 13.3.
[156]Ps 36.9.
[157]Matt 13.25.
[158]Ps 72.8, LXX, Luke 18.14.
[159]Ps 83.6, LXX.
[160]Luke 11.24.
[161]Mark 5.9–13, Luke 8.30–33.

the house from which it withdrew. It is shameless, it is contentious. Again it attacks, again it tries. If it finds that Christ has made his dwelling within and filled the place that it has itself emptied, it is again driven off, it departs without success, pitiful as it wanders around. But if it finds the place in you "swept and adorned,"[162] empty and unused, equally ready to receive whoever takes it first, it bursts in, enters and dwells there with a larger entourage. And "the last condition becomes worse than the first,"[163] inasmuch as then there was hope of correction and safety, but now the evil is manifest, the flight from the good attracts the bad, and because of this the inhabitant's possession is somehow more secure.

36 Again I will remind you of illuminations and will often gather examples of them from the divine Scriptures. For I myself will take pleasure in the memory of these things—for what is more pleasant than light to those who have tasted light?—and I will surround you with lightning flashes by my words. "Light has risen for the righteous"[164] and its companion, joy. "There is light for the just at all times."[165] "You illumine wondrously from the eternal mountains"[166] is said to God. It concerns the angelic powers, in my view, who work with us toward the good. "The Lord is my light and my savior; whom shall I fear?"[167] I have heard David say. And sometimes he asks God to send out his light and truth,[168] while at other times he gives thanks because he has indeed participated in this, in that the light of God is imprinted on him,[169] that is, the signs of the illumination given him are imprinted and made known. One light alone let us flee, the offspring of the cruel fire. Let us not walk in the light of our fire and

---

[162]Luke 11.25.
[163]Luke 11.26.
[164]Ps 96.11, LXX.
[165]Prov 13.9, LXX.
[166]Ps 76.4.
[167]Ps 26.1, LXX.
[168]Ps 43.3.
[169]Ps 4.6.

by the flame which we have kindled.[170] For I know also a purifying fire, which Christ came to cast upon the earth.[171] And he is himself called a fire in an anagogical sense.[172] This consumes matter and evil habits, and Christ wants to kindle it swiftly,[173] for he desires that we do good quickly, since he even gives us burning coals[174] as a help. I know also a fire that does not purify but indeed punishes: either the fire of Sodom, which the Lord rains down on all sinners mixed with brimstone and tempest;[175] or that prepared for the devil and his angels;[176] or that which goes forth before the face of the Lord and burns up his enemies all around;[177] and, what is even more fearful than these, that which does not rest and is deployed with the worm, which is not extinguished but remains forever for the wicked.[178] For all these fires belong to the destroying power, unless some prefer even here to understand this fire as showing more love to humankind, in a way worthy of the punisher.[179]

37 As I know a twofold fire, I also know a twofold light. The one is a lamp for our directive faculty, making straight our steps according to God. The other is deceptive and meddling and opposed to the true light while pretending to be that light, that it may defraud through its appearance. This is indeed darkness yet seems to be midday, the highest summit of light. This is how I read the text about those who continually flee the darkness at midday.[180] This also is night and is

---

[170]Isa 50.11.
[171]Luke 12.49.
[172]Deut 4.24.
[173]Luke 12.49–50.
[174]Rom 12.20.
[175]Gen 19.24, Ps 11.6.
[176]Matt 25.41.
[177]Ps 97.3.
[178]Mark 9.43, Isa 66.24.
[179]Gregory is saying that he considers universal salvation, which would follow as much purification as is needed after death, as a possibility. However, unlike his friend Gregory of Nyssa, whom he probably has in mind here, he stops short of affirming it as a necessary outcome of God's infinite goodness and patience with creaturely freedom.
[180]Isa 16.3, LXX.

considered illumination by those corrupted by luxury. For what does David say? "Night was around me, the wretched one, and I did not know it; for I supposed that luxury was illumination."[181] But such are they and this their condition. As for us, however, let us illumine ourselves with the light of knowledge. This is done by sowing unto justice[182] and harvesting the fruit of life, for action is the patron of contemplation, that among other things we may learn also what is the true light and what is the false, and may not fall unawares into evil perceived as good. Let us become light, as the disciples heard from the great Light, who said, "You are the light of the world."[183] Let us become lights in the world offering the word of life[184] that is a power of life for others. Let us receive divinity, let us receive the first and most undiluted Light. Let us walk toward his radiance before our feet stumble on dark and hostile mountains. While it is day, "let us walk honorably as in the day, not with reveling and drunkenness, not with lewdness and licentiousness,"[185] which are the thefts of the night.

38   Let us purify every limb and organ, brothers and sisters, let us sanctify every sense. Let there be nothing imperfect in us, nothing of the first birth; let us leave nothing unillumined. Let us illumine our eyes that we may look straight and not carry in ourselves any prostitute idol through busy and meddlesome sight. For even if we do not worship the passion, still we have defiled our soul. If there is any beam in us, or any splinter, let us clean it out completely, that we may also be able to see those of others.[186] Let us illumine our hearing, let us illumine our tongue, that we may hear what the Lord God will say,[187] and he will make us hear his mercy in the morning,[188] and

---

[181]Ps 138.11, LXX.
[182]Hos 10.12.
[183]Matt 5.14.
[184]Phil 2.15–16.
[185]Rom 13.13.
[186]Matt 7.3–5.
[187]Ps 85.8.
[188]Ps 143.10.

we will hear of joy and gladness,[189] which sound in godly ears. May we not be a sharp sword[190] or a sharpened razor,[191] or roll under our tongue trouble and sorrow,[192] but speak wisdom from God in a mystery, that which has been hidden,[193] respecting the fiery tongues.[194] Let us heal our sense of smell, that we may not be effeminate, nor covered with dust instead of pleasant fragrances.[195] Rather, let us rejoice, sharing spiritually in the perfume poured out[196] for our sake, and be so formed and transformed by it that the Lord also smells a pleasant fragrance from us.[197] Let us purify our touch, taste, and throat, not touching softly and enjoying smooth things, but touching[198] the Word made flesh for our sake as is fitting, and imitating Thomas[199] in this. Let us not have sauces and seasonings tickling our palate, since they are akin to more harmful ticklings. Rather, let us taste and know that the Lord is good,[200] a better and more lasting taste. Let us not refresh briefly that cruel and ungrateful conduit, which sends through and does not keep what has been given it. Rather, let us delight it with divine words sweeter than honey.[201]

39 Also, besides what has been said, it is again good for your head to be purified, as the head that is the workshop of the senses is purified, to hold fast the head of Christ, "from whom the whole body is fitted and joined together,"[202] and to throw down the sin that has raised itself above us, being raised up by what is better. It is good

[189]Ps 51.8.
[190]Ps 57.5.
[191]Ps 52.2.
[192]Ps 10.7.
[193]1 Cor 2.7.
[194]Acts 2.3.
[195]Isa 3.24.
[196]Song 1.3.
[197]Gen 8.21.
[198]1 John 1.1.
[199]John 20.25.
[200]Ps 34.8.
[201]Ps 19.10.
[202]Col 2.19.

also to sanctify and purify our shoulder, that we may be able to bear the cross of Christ, which is not easily borne by everybody. It is good for the hands to be made perfect and the feet, the hands so as to be lifted up holy in every place and to grasp the teaching of Christ, lest the Lord at any time be angry,[203] and that through action the word may be believed, which was given by the hand of the prophet;[204] the feet that they may not be swift to spill blood[205] or run to evil, but be prepared for the gospel[206] and for the prize of the upward calling[207] and receive Christ who washes and purifies them.[208] If there is also any purification for the stomach, which contains and digests the food from the Word, it is good also not to make it a god[209] through luxury and perishable food, but to purify it as much as possible and make it lighter, so as to receive the Word of the Lord in its midst and grieve[210] well over the stumbling of Israel. I find also the heart and the inward parts worthy of honor. And David persuades me of this, asking that a pure heart be created in him and an upright spirit renewed in his inward parts,[211] meaning, in my view, the rational faculty, and clearly also its movements and reasonings.

40 What about the loins? What about the kidneys? Let us not pass these by. Let the purification touch these also. Let our loins have a belt around them[212] and be restrained by continence, as Israel did of old, according to the Law, when participating in the Passover.[213] For nobody went forth from Egypt in purity or escaped the destroyer[214] without this discipline. And let our kidneys undergo

[203]Ps 2.12, LXX.
[204]Jer 50.1, Hag 1.1.
[205]Prov 1.16.
[206]Eph 6.15.
[207]Phil 3.14.
[208]John 13.5–10.
[209]Phil 3.19.
[210]Jer 4.19.
[211]Ps 51.10.
[212]Luke 12.35, Eph 6.14.
[213]Exod 12.11.
[214]Exod 11.4–6, 12.29.

the good change, transferring wholly to God their faculty of desire, so that we are able to say, "Lord, before you is all my desire,"[215] and, "I have not desired the day of a human being."[216] For it is necessary to become a "man of desires,"[217] those of the Spirit. Thus also we can destroy the dragon, which carries most of its strength in its navel and its loins,[218] if we mortify the power that comes to it from these places. And do not marvel if indeed I give more abundant honor to our unseemly parts,[219] mortifying them and making them chaste by my words, and standing against matter. Giving to God all "our limbs and organs that are on the earth,"[220] let us consecrate everything, not the lobe of the liver, or the kidneys with the fat, or some part of the body, or this or that. For why should we dishonor the rest? But let us offer the whole of ourselves, let us become reason-endowed whole burnt offerings,[221] perfect sacrifices, not setting aside for the priest only the shoulder or the breast,[222] for that is a small thing. Rather, in giving ourselves whole to God, let us receive in return the whole, since to receive purely is this, to be given to God and make our own salvation a sacred offering.

41   Besides all this and above all, guard for me the good deposit,[223] by which I live and by which I also govern, and which I desire to accompany me in my journey hence, with which I bear everything painful and spit upon every pleasure, the confession of Father and Son and Holy Spirit. I entrust this to you today. With this I will both submerge you [in the water] and raise you up. This I give you as a companion and protector for all your life, the one divinity and power, found in unity in the three, and gathering together the three

²¹⁵Ps 38.9.
²¹⁶Jer 17.16, LXX.
²¹⁷Dan 9.23, LXX.
²¹⁸Job 40.16, LXX.
²¹⁹1 Cor 12.23.
²²⁰Col 3.5.
²²¹Rom 12.1.
²²²Num 6.20, Lev 10.14–15.
²²³2 Tim 1.14.

as distinct; neither uneven in essences or natures, nor increased or decreased by superiorities or inferiorities; from every perspective equal, from every perspective the same, as the beauty and greatness of heaven is one; an infinite coalescence of three infinites; each God when considered[224] in himself; as the Father so the Son, as the Son so the Holy Spirit; each preserving his properties. The three are God when known together, each God because of the consubstantiality, one God because of the monarchy. When I first know the one I am also illumined from all sides by the three; when I first distinguish the three I am also carried back to the one. When I picture one of the three I consider this the whole, and my eyes are filled, and the greater part has escaped me. I cannot grasp the greatness of that one so as to grant something greater to the rest. When I bring the three together in contemplation, I see one torch and am unable to divide or measure the united light.

42 Do you fear the "generation," lest God undergo anything, he who is impassible?[225] I fear the "creation," lest I lose God through the insult and the unjust division, either cutting the Son away from the Father or cutting away from the Son the essence of the Spirit. For it is paradoxical, not only that creation is inserted into God by those who wrongly measure out the divinity, but that even the creation is cut off from itself. As indeed the Son is ranked below the Father by those who are base and lie below, so likewise the dignity of the Spirit is also ranked below that of the Son, as both God and creation are insulted by this new theology. Nothing in the Trinity, my friends, is a slave or a creature, or is introduced from outside, as I heard one of the wise say. "If I still pleased humans, I would not be a slave of Christ,"[226] says the divine apostle. If I still worshipped a creature or was baptized into a creature, I would not be divinized, nor would

---

[224]The Greek word also means "contemplated."

[225]In this paragraph, Gregory is arguing against Arian or Eunomian opponents who believe that the Son is created and is inferior to the Father.

[226]Gal 1.10.

I have transformed my first birth. What shall I say to those who worship Astarte, or Chemosh,[227] the abomination of the Sidonians, or the image of a star—a god a little above these according to the idolators, but still created and made—if I myself do not worship the two into whom I have been conjointly baptized, or else worship my fellow slaves? For [according to my opponents] they are fellow slaves, even if a little more honorable, since also among fellow slaves there exists a kind of distinction and preeminence?

43 I would like to say the Father is "greater,"[228] from whom indeed equality and being come to those who are equal, for this is granted by everybody. And I fear to call him the origin, lest I make him the origin of inferiors and insult him through this preeminence; for it is not glory to the one from whom they come to abase those who come from him. Moreover, I suspect you are insatiable, and that taking the "greater" you would cut the nature in two, using the word "greater" in every sense. For the "greater" does not apply to the nature but to the cause. For nothing of those who are one in essence is greater or less in essence. I would like to give the Son preeminence over the Spirit, as Son, but baptism does not concede it to me, which perfects me through the Spirit. But do you fear being reproached for tri-the-ism? You keep the prize, that is the unity in the three, but leave to me the battle. Let me be the shipbuilder, you use the ship. And if another is the shipbuilder, accept me as master builder of the house; you dwell there in safety, though you did not labor at all. You will not have a less successful voyage or dwell less in the house if it is I who constructed them and you have not labored on them. See how great my kindheartedness is? See the goodness of the Spirit? Mine will be the war, yours the reward of victory. Let me be under fire, but you be at peace, praying with the one who fights for you; and give me your hand through the faith. I have three stones to sling against the Philistine.[229] I have three breaths for the son of the woman of

227Num 21.29, 1 Kgs 11.7.
228John 14.28.
2291 Sam 17.40–49. David had five stones.

Zarephath, by which I will give life to the dead.[230] I have three floods for the firewood, to consecrate the sacrifice, kindling fire with water, the greatest paradox; and I will strike down the prophets of shame, using the power of mystery.[231]

44 What need do I have for longer speeches? For it is the time for teachings, not controversies. "I testify before God and the elect angels,"[232] that you must be baptized with this faith. If anyone has written in you in a way other than my discourse demands, come and have the writing changed. I am not without talent as a calligrapher of these things, writing what has been written in me and teaching what I have been taught and have kept from the beginning to these gray hairs. Mine is the danger, mine also the privilege as the director of your soul and the one who perfects you through baptism. And if you hold these beliefs and have been marked with the good writing, guard for me what has been written and remain unchanging in changing times about the unchanging reality. Imitate Pilate in a better way, who wrote badly while you have been written upon well. Say to those who would persuade you otherwise, "What I have written, I have written."[233] For indeed I would be ashamed if while the bad remains unbending the good very easily bends aside. It is necessary to be easily moved toward the better from the worse, but unmoved toward the worse from the better. If you are baptized thus and according to this teaching, "see, I will not restrain my lips";[234] see, I lend my hands to the Spirit. Let us hasten salvation, let us rise and go to baptism; the Spirit is eager, the initiator is willing, the gift is prepared. But if you still limp[235] and do not receive the Divinity in its perfection, look for another to baptize you, or to drown you. I do not have the leisure to cut [apart] the Divinity and make you dead at

[230] 1 Kgs 17.21–22.
[231] 1 Kgs 18.34–40.
[232] 1 Tim 5.21.
[233] John 19.22.
[234] Ps 40.9.
[235] 1 Kgs 18.21.

the time of your rebirth, so that you might have neither the grace nor the hope of grace, and in a short time shipwreck your salvation.[236] For whichever of the three you stole from the Divinity, the whole would be destroyed, and so would your initiation.

45   However, nothing has yet been inscribed in your soul, neither bad nor good writing, and you need us to write on you today and mark you with a view to perfection. Let us enter within the cloud.[237] Give me the tablets[238] of your heart. I am becoming Moses for you, even if it is bold to say it. I am writing with the finger of God a new decalogue,[239] I am writing a summary of salvation. But if there is some heretical and irrational beast, let it remain below, or it risks being stoned[240] by the word of truth. I will baptize you, instructing you in the name of the Father and the Son and the Holy Spirit. And the name common to the three is one, that is the Divinity. And you will know both by rites and by words, that as you reject the whole of atheism, you are allied with the whole of the Divinity.

Believe that the whole universe, all that is visible and all that is invisible, was brought into being out of nothing by God and is governed by the providence of its Creator, and will receive a change to a better condition. Believe that evil has neither substance nor sovereignty, nor is it without beginning, nor does it have its own subsistence, nor does it come from God. Rather, it is our work and that of the Evil One, and it was introduced by our inattention, not by that of the Creator. Believe that the Son of God, the Word before the ages, begotten from the Father apart from time and without body, has in the last days also become for you Son of a human being, coming forth from the Virgin Mary ineffably and in an undefiled manner, for there is no defilement where God is and in the way through which salvation comes. He is a whole human being, and the same [person]

[236] 1 Tim 1.19.
[237] Exod 24.18.
[238] Exod 31.18.
[239] Exod 20.3–17.
[240] Exod 19.12–13.

is also God, on behalf of the whole sufferer, that salvation may be granted to the whole of you, destroying the whole condemnation of sin. He is impassible in his divinity, passible in what he has assumed. He is as much human for your sake as you may become god because of him. He, for our iniquities, was led to death, was crucified and buried, as far as to taste death, and rose again on the third day and ascended into the heavens, to bring with him you who lie below. He will come again with his glorious presence, judging the living and the dead, no longer flesh yet not without body but, according to the principles he himself knows, with a more deiform body, that he may be seen by those who have pierced him[241] and also remain God without fleshly coarseness. Accept besides these things resurrection, judgment, and recompense according to the just balances of God. And this will be light to those whose mind has been purified, that is God seen and known, in proportion to each one's purity, which indeed we also call the kingdom of heaven. However, it will be darkness to those blinded in their directive faculty, that is estrangement from God, in proportion to their dimness of sight here. Tenth, do good work[242] on this foundation of dogmas, since "faith without works is dead,"[243] as are works without faith. You now have what can be divulged of the mystery and what is not forbidden to the ears of the multitude. And the rest you will learn inside, by the grace of the Trinity, which also you will conceal in yourself, guarded by a seal.

46 But I announce this good news to you. The position in which you will stand immediately after baptism before the great sanctuary[244] is a foreshadowing of the future glory. The psalmody with which you will be received is a prelude of the hymnody there. The

[241]Rev 1.7, John 19.37, Zech 12.10.

[242]Gal 6.10.

[243]Jas 2.17.

[244]Literally, "bema." The bema is a platform at the front of the church, a few steps up from where the congregation usually stands. The clergy stand on the bema during services. In Gregory's church, the newly baptized must have been invited to stand there after they processed together from the baptistery into the church.

lamps that you will kindle are a symbol of the procession of lights there, with which you will go to meet the Bridegroom with bright and virgin souls,[245] with lamps bright with faith. Let us not lie down in laziness, lest we miss the unexpected presence of the Expected One. Let us not lack food and oil and good works, lest we be thrown out of the bridal chamber. For I see how pitiful the suffering is. He will be present when the cry demands the meeting, and of those who come to meet him, some who are wise will have lamps alight and abundant fuel for them, while others are troubled seeking oil at the wrong time from those who have it. He will enter swiftly, and the first will enter with him, but the others will be shut out, having spent the time for entry on preparations; and afterwards they will weep much, learning too late the damage caused by laziness, when the bridal chamber is no longer accessible to them despite their many pleadings, since they wickedly closed it for themselves. They will have imitated in another way those who miss the wedding feast that the good Father gives for the good Bridegroom,[246] one because of the wife he has newly married, another because of the field he has newly bought, and another because of the yoke of oxen he has unfortunately acquired, since for the sake of smaller things they lose greater things. For not one is there of the disdainful or the lazy or those dressed in filthy rags and not in wedding attire, even if here he considers himself worthy of the bright attire there and secretly inserts himself,[247] thoroughly deceiving himself by empty hopes. What then? When we come inside, then the Bridegroom knows what he will teach and how he will be joined with the souls that have come in with him. He will be joined with them, in my view, in teaching them things most perfect and most pure. May we also participate in that who are teaching these things and learning them, in the same Christ our Lord, to whom be glory unto the ages. Amen.

[245]Matt 25.1–13.
[246]Luke 14.16–24.
[247]Matt 22.11–13.

On Pentecost

1   Let us reflect briefly about the feast, that we may keep the feast spiritually. For others there are other celebrations; but for the servant of the Word there is a discourse, and among words there are those most suitable to the occasion. And one who loves good things rejoices no less in the good than one who loves feasts rejoices in celebrating spiritually. Let us consider the matter as follows. The Jew also keeps feasts, but in accord with the letter; while pursuing the bodily law, he has not attained the spiritual law. The Greek also keeps feasts, but in accord with the body and his own gods and demons, of whom some are fashioners of passions, as they themselves admit, while others are honored by passions. For this reason, even their keeping of feasts is passionate in that sinning honors the divinity, toward whom the passion flees for refuge as if it were something venerable. As for us, we also keep feast, but as is pleasing to the Spirit. And he is pleased that we speak or act in accord with some duty. And for us to keep a feast is this, to treasure up for the soul some things that are stable and sovereign, but not those that withdraw and are dissolved and flatter the senses a little but are, in my judgment, mostly destructive and harmful. For its own evil is sufficient for the body.[1] But why must one give more fuel to the flame or more abundant food to the beast, so that it becomes harder to restrain and more violent against reason?

2   For these reasons, then, let us keep feast spiritually. And this is the beginning of our speech—for we must speak even if our speech

---

[1]Matt 6.34.

digresses a little, and we must labor for those who love speeches that we may, as it were, mix in some seasoning with the celebration. The children of the Hebrews honor the number seven following the legislation of Moses, just as later the Pythagoreans honored the number four by which also they made oaths; and the followers of Simon and Marcion honored the numbers eight and thirty, to which indeed they attached an equal number of aeons, which they honored.[2] I do not know what their principles of analogy are or what power this number has, but they honor it.

Yet it is clear that in six days God produced and shaped matter and adorned it with varied and complex forms and created this present visible world,[3] then on the seventh day rested from his works,[4] as also the name "sabbath" makes clear, which in Hebrew means "rest." But if anyone has a more exalted explanation of these matters, let others study it.

Yet the honor is not for these days alone but also extends to years. Thus among days the sabbath[5] is that which they continually honor, just as likewise the removal of leaven[6] is for the same number of days; and among years the seventh is the year of release.[7] And this concerns not only sevens but sevens of sevens, alike in days and years. Thus the sevens of days generate Pentecost[8] which is called by them a holy day;[9] the sevens of years to what they call Jubilee, which brings all at once release of land, freedom for slaves and release of property bought.[10] For this people consecrates to God not only the

[2]Many people in the ancient world were fascinated with number symbolism, including Jews, Greek philosophers and Gnostic teachers as well as church fathers such as Gregory. Note that he seems to have confused Marcion with Valentinus, who believed in a divine realm containing thirty aeons, or a similar Gnostic teacher.

[3]Gen 1.1–31.
[4]Gen 2.3.
[5]Exod 20.8–10, 31.14–17.
[6]Exod 12.15.
[7]Lev 25.4.
[8]"Pentecost" is a form of the Greek word for "fifty" and thus names the fiftieth day after Pascha.
[9]Lev 23.21.
[10]Lev 25.8ff.

firstfruits of offspring or the firstborn but also the firstfruits of days and years.

Thus the honoring of the number seven brought with it the honor of Pentecost. For seven multiplied by itself generates fifty minus one day, and this we have taken from the age to come, which is at once the eighth and the first, or rather one and indissoluble. For the present sabbath of souls must cease in the age to come as a portion of the seven is given and of the eight,[11] as some of those before us have already understood the text of Solomon.

3 There are many testimonies to the number seven's honor, but of the many a few are sufficient for us. Honorable spirits are named as seven; they are, in my view, the energies of the Spirit, which Isaiah likes to call "spirits."[12] "The words of the Lord are," according to David, "purified sevenfold";[13] and the righteous one is "delivered six times from tribulations, and the seventh time is not stricken."[14] The sinner is pardoned not only seven times, but even seventy times seven times.[15] Yet again there is testimony from opposites—for the punishment of evil is also praiseworthy—"Cain is avenged seven times,"[16] that is a penalty was exacted from him for his fratricide; but Lamech "seventy times seven times,"[17] since he was a murderer after the law and the condemnation. The wicked neighbors receive "sevenfold into their bosom";[18] and the house of wisdom rests on seven pillars;[19] and the same number of eyes adorn the stone of Zerubbabel.[20] God is praised "seven times a day."[21] And indeed "the

---

[11]Eccl 11.2.
[12]Isa 11.2, LXX.
[13]Ps 12.6.
[14]Job 5.19.
[15]Matt 18.21–22.
[16]Gen 4.15–24.
[17]Gen 4.24.
[18]Ps 79.12.
[19]Prov 9.1.
[20]Zech 3.9.
[21]Ps 119.164.

barren woman bears seven children,"[22] the perfect number in contrast to the one who is imperfect in her children.

4 If one must also examine the ancient histories, I note that the seventh of the forefathers, Enoch, has been honored by translation.[23] I note also that the twenty-first, Abraham, was glorified as a patriarch by the addition of a greater mystery,[24] for three times seven makes this number. And if one is among those who have youth's boldness in everything, one might also come to the new Adam,[25] my God and Lord Jesus Christ, who is numbered as the seventy-seventh after the old Adam who was under sin, according to Luke's backward genealogy.[26] I note also the seven trumpets of Joshua son of Nun and the same number of circuits and days and priests by which the walls of Jericho were shaken down.[27] So also there are the seven turnings of Elijah the prophet, by which he breathed life into the widow of Zarephath's son[28] and an equal number of floodings of wood, when by fire sent from God the same prophet consumed the sacrifice and condemned the prophets of shame, who were unable to equal this at his challenge.[29] Thus also the seven searches for a cloud required of his young servant,[30] and Elisha bending the same number of times over the son of the Shunamite, rekindling life in him by breath.[31] The principle is the same, in my view, not only in the seven branches and seven lamps of the temple's candlestick,[32] but also in the priest's initiation in seven days,[33] the leper's cleansing in seven days,[34] and

[22] 1 Sam 2.5.
[23] Gen 5.3–24.
[24] Gen 5.3–30, 10.21–24, 11.10–27.
[25] 1 Cor 15.45.
[26] Luke 3.23–28.
[27] Josh 6.3–10.
[28] 1 Kgs 17.18–22.
[29] 1 Kgs 18.25–40. There were three floodings, not seven.
[30] 1 Kgs 18.43–44.
[31] 4 Kgdms 4.35, LXX; Hebrew: 2 Kgs 4.35.
[32] Exod 25.31–37.
[33] Cf. Lev 8.33, Exod 29.20.
[34] Lev 14.37–39.

the temple's dedication in the same number of days.[35] And in the seventieth year the people returned from captivity,[36] that what is the case for ones may also become so for tens, and that the mystery of seven may be honored by a more perfect number. But why do I speak of distant events? Jesus himself, the pure perfection, knew how to feed five thousand in the desert even with five loaves,[37] and again he knew how to feed four thousand with seven.[38] And the leftovers of those filled here were twelve baskets[39] and there seven baskets.[40] None of these things, in my view, is without reason or unworthy of the Spirit. And if you total them up for yourself you will observe many numbers that have a meaning deeper than what appears. But what is most useful on the present occasion is that—perhaps for these reasons or others close to them, or reasons more divine—the Hebrews honor the day of Pentecost, and we honor it also; just as there are certain other observances of the Hebrews, kept by them typologically but reestablished by us mystically. Having spoken beforehand of so many matters concerning the day, let us go on in our discourse to what follows.

5   We celebrate Pentecost and the dwelling with us of the Spirit and the appointed time of promise[41] and the fulfillment of hope. The mystery is as great as it is venerable. What concerns Christ's embodiment is ended, or rather what concerns his bodily dwelling with us; for I hesitate to speak of bodily matters as long as no argument persuades me that it is good to put aside the body. What concerns the Spirit is beginning. And what concerned Christ? A virgin, birth, a manger, wrapping in swaddling clothes, angels glorifying him, shepherds running to him, a star in motion, magi worshiping him and bearing

[35]1 Kgs 8.65.
[36]Jer 25.11, 29.10; 2 Chr 36.21.
[37]Matt 14.19–21, Mark 6.41–44, Luke 9.16, John 6.9–11.
[38]Matt 15.36–38, Mark 8.6–9.
[39]Matt 14.20, Mark 6.43, Luke 9.17, John 6.13.
[40]Matt 15.37, Mark 8.8.
[41]John 14.16, 26, 15.26, 16.7.

gifts, Herod's murder of children, Jesus fleeing into Egypt and returning from Egypt, circumcised, baptized, receiving testimony from
above, tempted, stoned[42] for our sake—by which he had to be given
as a model of suffering on behalf of the word[43]—betrayed, nailed to
the cross, buried, risen, ascended. Many things he suffers even now:
dishonors from the haters of Christ—and he bears them, for he is
longsuffering,—honors from the friends of Christ. And as he delays
his anger toward the first, so also he delays his kindness toward us;
toward them probably to give an opportunity for repentance, and
toward us to test our desire, to see if we are faint-hearted in our
tribulations and struggles on behalf of piety. From the beginning, this
indeed was the principle of the divine plan and his incomprehensible
judgments,[44] by which he wisely directs our affairs. Such indeed are
the things concerning Christ; and what follows we will see to be more
glorious, and may we too be seen. As for what concerns the Spirit,
may the Spirit assist me and give me speech, as much as I would like;
but if not that much, as much as is fitting to the occasion. And he will
assist entirely as a master, but not as a slave, not awaiting a command,
as some suppose. For he blows where he wills, and upon whom, and
whenever and however much he wishes. Thus are we inspired both
to think and to speak about the Spirit.

6 Those who bring the Holy Spirit down to the level of a creature
are insolent and wicked slaves and wickedest of the wicked. For it is
wicked slaves who push aside authority and rebel against sovereignty
and make the free person a fellow slave to themselves. Those who
regard him as God are divinely inspired and have radiant minds.
And those who also name him as such are exalted if speaking to
the wise. But if speaking to the base, they are not prudent but are
entrusting a pearl to the mud and the sound of thunder to injured

---

[42]John 8.19.

[43]At an earlier point during his brief ministry in Constantinople, enemies
attempted to stone Gregory.

[44]Rom 11.33.

ears and the sun to weakened eyes and solid food to those still given milk to drink.[45] It is necessary to lead them forward little by little to what is in front of them and guide them onward to the higher things, giving light by light and offering truth by truth. Therefore we also, giving up for a while the more perfect discourse—for it is not yet the time—speak of him thus.

7 If, my friends, you do not recognize the Holy Spirit as uncreated, nor as eternal, this is clearly the activity of the contrary spirit. Grant to my zeal a little overboldness. But if you are of sound enough mind to flee manifest impiety and place outside of slavery the one who indeed makes us free, examine what follows for yourself, with the Holy Spirit and with us. For I am persuaded that you have some participation in the Spirit and as our kin are already examining the question with us. Either show me the midpoint between slavery and lordship, that I may place the Holy Spirit there, or if you flee slavery, there is no doubt about where to rank the one we seek. Yet you are distressed by the syllables and trip over the word,[46] and this becomes for you a stone of stumbling and a rock of offense,[47] as Christ also is for some.[48] It is human weakness. Let us agree with each other about the Spirit, let us love our brothers rather that loving ourselves. Grant the power of divinity and we will grant you a concession regarding the word; confess the nature through other words that you respect more, and we will heal you as sick persons for whom one secretly concedes some pleasures. For it is shameful, shameful and truly irrational, to be healthy in soul but quibble about the sound and hide the treasure, as if begrudging it to others, or fearing lest you sanctify your tongue also. Yet it is more shameful for us to suffer that of which we accuse you and condemn your quibbling while ourselves quibbling about the letters.

[45] 1 Cor 3.2.
[46] The word is probably "God" or "*homoousios*."
[47] Isa 8.14.
[48] Rom 9.33.

8   Confess, my friends, the Trinity as one divinity, and, if you will, one nature; and we will ask the Spirit to give you the word "God." For I know well, he who gives the first will give also the second, and especially if the conflict is about a certain spiritual cowardice, not a diabolical plot. I will speak still more clearly and briefly. Do not call us to account for the more exalted word—for envy has nothing to do with this ascent—and we will not bring charges against what you have attained thus far, until you also are brought by another road to the same inn. For we do not seek to conquer but to gain brothers, by whose separation we are torn apart. We say these things to you in whom also we find something alive, to you who are of sound mind regarding the Son, whose life we admire though we do not entirely approve your language. You who have the things of the Spirit, receive also the Spirit himself, that you may not only struggle but also struggle lawfully, from which also comes the crown.[49] May this be granted you as a reward for your way of life, to confess the Spirit perfectly and proclaim him with us and before us, as far as is fitting. I dare also to say something greater in your behalf, in the words of the Apostle. I am so attached to you and have so much respect for your modest clothing and the color of your self-restraint and your holy assemblies and noble virginity and purity and psalmody through the whole night and love for the poor and brothers and strangers, that I would even accept to be anathema from Christ[50] and suffer something as one condemned, if only you would stand with us and we could glorify the Trinity together. As for the others, what indeed must I say? They are clearly dead, whom Christ alone can raise, who gives life to the dead by his own power. Are they not badly separated in place though bound together in doctrine, while they struggle as much against each other as squinting eyes looking at one object and differing not in their vision but in its placement, if indeed we may charge them with squinting and not blindness?

[49] 2 Tim 2.10.
[50] Rom 9.3.

Since I have set these matters before you sufficiently, come, let us return again to the Spirit, and I think you will also follow me now.

9 The Holy Spirit always was and is and will be, without beginning, without end, but is always ranked and numbered with the Father and the Son. For it was not at any time fitting that the Son be lacking to the Father, or the Spirit to the Son. For it would have been the greatest dishonor for the divinity to have come, as it were, through a change of mind to a fullness of perfection. Hence the Spirit always is participated in[51] but does not participate, perfects but is not perfected, fills[52] but is not filled, sanctifies[53] but is not sanctified, deifies[54] but is not deified. He is always the same as himself and as those with whom he is ranked, invisible, eternal, uncontainable, unchanging,[55] without quality, without quantity, without form, intangible, self-moving, ever-moving, self-determining,[56] self-powered,[57] all-powerful.[58] If indeed this pertains to the first cause, as it is all ascribed to the Only-begotten so it is also ascribed to the Spirit. He is life and creates life,[59] he is light and distributes light,[60] he is the goodness itself[61] and source of goodness. He is the upright Spirit,[62] sovereign,[63] Lord;[64] he sends,[65] sets apart,[66] builds a temple[67] for

[51]1 Cor 6.11.
[52]Wis 1.7.
[53]1 Cor 6.11.
[54]1 Cor 3.16–17, 6.19; 2 Cor 6.16.
[55]Wis 7.23.
[56]Wis 7.23.
[57]2 Cor 3.17.
[58]Wis 7.23.
[59]John 6.63.
[60]John 14.26.
[61]Ps 142.10.
[62]Ps 50.12, LXX.
[63]Ps 50.14, LXX.
[64]2 Cor 3.17.
[65]Acts 13.4.
[66]Acts 13.2.
[67]1 Cor 3.16, 6.19; 2 Cor 6.16.

himself, guides,[68] acts as he wills, distributes gifts.[69] He is the Spirit of adoption,[70] of truth,[71] of wisdom, of understanding, of knowledge, of piety, of counsel, of strength, of fear, as was enumerated,[72] through whom the Father is known and the Son glorified,[73] and by whom alone he is known. They are one common rank, one in adoration, worship, power, perfection, sanctification. Why should I speak at length? All that belongs to the Father belongs to the Son except unbegottenness. All that belongs to the Son belongs to the Spirit except begottenness. These things do not divide the essence, according to my teaching, but they are divided in the [common] essence.

10   Are you in labor to bring forth objections? I am too to get on with my discourse. Honor the day of the Spirit. Hold back your tongue a little, if you can. Our discourse is about other tongues;[74] respect them or fear them, seeing that they are of fire. Today let us teach, tomorrow let us quibble; today let us keep feast, tomorrow let us behave rudely. This is mystical, that is theatrical. This is for the churches, that is for the marketplaces. This is for the sober, that is for the drunk. This is for the serious, that is for those who poke fun at the Spirit.

And now that we have pushed aside what is foreign, come, let us fully establish what is our own.

11   The Spirit acted first in the angelic and heavenly powers, and in those who are first after God and are around God. For it is not from elsewhere that they possess their perfection and their illumination, and their difficulty or impossibility of moving toward evil, but from the Holy Spirit. Then he acted in the patriarchs and in the prophets;

[68]Ps 142.10, Isa 63.14.
[69]1 Cor 12.11.
[70]Rom 8.15.
[71]John 14.17, 15.26.
[72]Isa 11.2, LXX.
[73]John 16.14.
[74]Acts 2.3.

the first saw God in an image or knew him, the others even foreknew the future, as the Spirit imprinted on the directive faculty of their souls, and associated with future events as if they were present, for such is the Spirit's power. Then he acted in the disciples of Christ—for I leave aside speaking of Christ, to whom he is present not by his action but as accompanying one equal in honor—and this in three ways, to the extent they were able to receive him, and on three occasions, before Christ was glorified by his passion, after he was glorified by his resurrection, and after his ascension to heaven, or his restoration or whatever it should be called. This is manifest first in purification of the sick and of spirits,[75] which quite clearly would not have happened without the Holy Spirit, and also the inbreathing after the resurrection,[76] which plainly is a more divine inspiration, and now the distribution of fiery tongues,[77] which indeed we are celebrating. However, the first manifested him indistinctly, the second more expressly, and the present one more perfectly, since he is no longer present [only] by an energy as at first, but in essence, if one may speak thus, coming to be with them and living with them. For it was fitting, since the Son associated with us corporeally, that the Spirit also should appear corporeally; and after Christ ascended again to his own place, that he should descend to us, coming in that he is Lord,[78] and sent[79] in that he is not a rival god. For such words show the harmony no less than the separation of natures.

12 Because of this, he came after Christ, that we might not lack an Advocate; but "another"[80] Advocate, that you might consider him of equal honor. For "other" signifies "another self," and this name indicates shared sovereignty, not dishonor. For I know that "other" is said not about those things that are different in kind

[75]Matt 10.1, Mark 3.15, Luke 9.1.
[76]John 20.22.
[77]Acts 2.3.
[78]John 16.8.
[79]John 14.16–17.
[80]John 14.16.

but about those that are one in essence. He comes in tongues[81] because of his kinship with the Word. And they are fiery;[82] I wonder whether this is because of the purification, for our Scripture knows also a purifying fire, as one who wishes can learn from many texts,[83] or because of his essence. For our God is fire,[84] and a fire consuming wickedness—though you may again be irritated, being confined by the oneness of essence. And the tongues were distributed[85] because of the diversity of gifts; and they rested on each[86] because of his royal dignity and his resting upon the saints, since also the Cherubim are the throne of God.[87] And this happened in an upper chamber[88]—if I do not appear to be more elaborate than I should—because of the ascent of those who would receive the gift and their lifting up from the earth, since also certain upper chambers are covered with divine waters through which God is praised in song.[89] And Jesus himself in an upper chamber gave communion in the Mystery to those being initiated into the higher realities, to show by this on the one hand that God must descend to us, as I know happened formerly to Moses,[90] and on the other hand that we must ascend, and thus there will be a communion of God with human beings by a coalescing of dignity. As long as each remains at his own level, the one at the top,[91] the other in lowliness, the goodness is not mingled and the love for humankind is not shared, and a great chasm that cannot be crossed[92] is in the middle, not only separating the rich man from Lazarus and the

[81] Acts 2.3.
[82] Ibid.
[83] Ps 11.7, LXX; 66.10; Mal 3.2–3.
[84] Deut 4.24.
[85] Acts 2.3.
[86] Ibid.
[87] Ps 79.2; Isa 37.16.
[88] Acts 1.13, 2.1.
[89] Ps 103.13.
[90] Exod 3.8, 19.18.
[91] Ps 14.2, 53.2.
[92] Luke 16.26.

longed-for bosom of Abraham,[93] but also the created and changing nature from that which is uncreated and stable.

13   The Spirit has been proclaimed by the prophets, as in the texts, "the Spirit of the Lord is upon me, because he has anointed me,"[94] and, "On him rested seven spirits,"[95] and, "The Spirit of the Lord descended and guided them";[96] and the Spirit of knowledge filled Bezaleel, the master builder of the tabernacle.[97] And the Spirit was provoked to anger;[98] and the Spirit lifted Elijah in a chariot and was sought in double measure by Elisha;[99] and David was guided and established by the good and ruling Spirit.[100] And long ago he was promised by Joel: "And it will be in the last days," he says, "I will pour out of my Spirit upon all flesh"—clearly the faithful—"and upon your sons and upon your daughters," and what follows;[101] later he was also promised by Jesus,[102] who is glorified by him and glorifies him in return,[103] just as he glorifies the Father and is glorified by the Father.[104] And how abundant the promise is! He will abide forever[105] and remain, either now with those who at this time are worthy, or later with those who become worthy of the things to come, when we have guarded the Holy Spirit intact by our way of life and not rejected him to the extent that we sin.

14   This Spirit fashions together with the Son both the creation and the resurrection. Be persuaded by these texts: "By the Word of the

[93]Luke 16.23.
[94]Isa 61.1.
[95]Isa 11.2.
[96]Isa 63.14.
[97]Exod 35.30–36.
[98]Isa 63.10.
[99]2 Kgs 2.11, 19.
[100]Ps 143.10; 50.14, LXX.
[101]Joel 2.28.
[102]John 14.16.
[103]John 16.13–14.
[104]John 8.54.
[105]John 14.16.

Lord the heavens were established, and by the Spirit of his mouth all their power";[106] "The divine Spirit created me, and the breath of the Almighty taught me";[107] and again, "You will send forth your Spirit and they will be created, and you will renew the face of the earth."[108] He also fashions the spiritual rebirth. Be persuaded by the text: "Nobody can see the kingdom or receive it unless he has been born from above by the Spirit,"[109] unless he has been purified from his earlier birth, which is a mystery of the night, by a molding in the day and in the light, through which each is molded by his own choice.

This Spirit, who is most wise and most loving toward humankind, if he takes a shepherd makes him a harper subduing evil spirits by song and proclaims him king of Israel.[110] If he takes a goatherd scraping mulberry trees, he makes him a prophet.[111] Consider David and Amos. If he takes a youth with natural talents, he makes him a judge of elders, even beyond his years.[112] Daniel testifies to this, who was victorious over lions in their den.[113] If he finds fishermen, he catches them in a net for Christ, they who catch the whole world with the line of the Word.[114] Take for me Peter and Andrew and the sons of thunder,[115] thundering the things of the Spirit. If he finds tax collectors, he gains them as disciples and makes them merchants of souls. Matthew says this,[116] who yesterday was a tax collector and today is an evangelist. If he finds fervent persecutors, he relocates their zeal and makes Pauls instead of Sauls and binds them to piety as much as they had been bound to evil.[117]

[106] Ps 33.6.
[107] Job 33.4, LXX.
[108] Ps 101.10.
[109] John 3.3–5.
[110] 1 Sam 16.12–23.
[111] Amos 7.14.
[112] Sus 45–60.
[113] Dan 6.17–23.
[114] Matt 4.18–22, Mark 1.16–17.
[115] Mark 3.17.
[116] Matt 9.9.
[117] Acts 9.3–22.

This Spirit also is most gentle yet is provoked to anger at sinners. Therefore, let us make his acquaintance as meek, not as wrathful, by confessing his dignity and fleeing blasphemy, and not choosing to see him implacably wrathful.[118]

He also has made me today a bold herald to you. If I do not suffer anything, thanks be to God; but if I do suffer, thanks even so; in the one case that he may spare those who hate us, and in the other that he may sanctify us by granting us to receive this reward for the ministry of the gospel, to be made perfect through blood.

15 They spoke in foreign tongues and not that of their fathers,[119] and, a great marvel, a language spoken by those not taught to speak it, and a sign for unbelievers, not for those who believe,[120] that by this would come an accusation against unbelievers, as indeed it is written, "In other tongues and by other lips I will speak to this people, and even so they will not give heed to me, says the Lord."[121] And "they heard."[122] Stop here a little and ask how to divide the text. For the reading has a certain ambiguity that is resolved by the punctuation. Did each, then, hear in his own language, as if to say one voice sounded forth but many were heard, so that the air resounded and, to say it more clearly, the voice became voices? Or after "they heard" is there a pause, while "speaking in their own languages"[123] is attached to what follows, so that it would be "speaking in languages" that belonged to the hearers, which had become "foreign"? I prefer to put it this way, for in the other interpretation the miracle could concern the hearers rather than the speakers, but in this interpretation it concerns the speakers, who indeed were accused of being drunk,[124] since clearly they worked a miracle with their voices by the Spirit.

[118]Matt 12.31–32.
[119]Acts 2.4.
[120]1 Cor 14.22.
[121]1 Cor 14.21, Isa 28.11.
[122]Acts 2.6.
[123]Ibid.
[124]Acts 2.13.

16   To be sure, the ancient division of tongues is praiseworthy—when those who in wickedness and impiety spoke the same language built the tower,[125] as even now some dare to do—for the dividing of languages broke apart their oneness of intention and destroyed their undertaking. Yet the present miracle is more praiseworthy. For being poured from one Spirit into many,[126] the divided tongues bring them together again into one accord.[127] And there is a diversity of gifts[128] that need another gift to distinguish which is better, since all possess what is praiseworthy. And one could say that that division is good of which David says, "Drown, Lord, and divide their tongues."[129] Why? Because "they loved every drowning word, a deceitful tongue."[130] He all but manifestly reproaches the present tongues that cut apart the divinity. But enough about this.

17   And since it was to the inhabitants of Jerusalem, to most devout Jews, Parthians and Medes, and Elamites, Egyptians and Libyans, Cretans and Arabs, Mesopotamians and my own Cappadocians,[131] that the tongues spoke, and to Jews from all nations under heaven,[132] and who—if one would like to understand it thus—had gathered there, it is worthwhile to see who they were and from what captivity they came. For the captivity in Egypt and Babylon was limited and long ago was ended by the return. The captivity under the Romans had not yet happened but would come, since it was a penalty for the audacity against the Savior. The captivity under Antiochus remains to be considered, which is not much earlier than these events. But if anyone does not accept this interpretation, regarding it as too elaborate—for this captivity was neither old, nor spread throughout much

[125]Gen 11.1–9.
[126]Acts 2.4.
[127]Acts 4.32.
[128]1 Cor 12.4.
[129]Ps 54.10, LXX.
[130]Ps 51.6, LXX.
[131]Acts 2.5, 9–11.
[132]Acts 2.5.

of the world—and seeks a more plausible one, perhaps it would be better to consider that many times and under many enemies the people were removed from their country, as Ezra recounts.[133] Some tribes returned safely, but some were left behind. Probably some of those scattered among many nations were present at that time and participated in the miracle.

18 These things have been examined before by those who want to learn, probably not without purpose. And whatever else anyone contributes to the present day, he also will be joined to us. But now we must dissolve the gathering, for the discourse is sufficient, but never the feast. But it is necessary to celebrate, now indeed in a bodily manner, and a little later in a wholly spiritual manner, where also we will know the reasons for these things more purely and more clearly, in the Word himself, our Lord and God Jesus Christ, in the true feast and joy of the saved. With him be glory and reverence to the Father with the Holy Spirit, now and unto the ages. Amen.

[133] 2 Esd 9.7, 11.8, LXX; Hebrew: Ezra 9.7, Neh 1.8.

On Holy Pascha

1 "I will stand on my watch," says the wondrous Habakkuk;[1] and I also will stand with him today, by the authority and vision given me by the Spirit, and I will look steadily and observe what will be seen and what will be spoken to me. I have stood and looked steadily, and behold a man mounted upon the clouds, and he was very exalted; and his appearance was like the appearance of an angel; and his raiment was like the brightness of lightning;[2] and he was lifting up his hand toward the east and shouting in a great voice.[3] His voice was like the voice of a trumpet; and those surrounding him were as a multitude of the heavenly hosts, and he said, "Today salvation has come to the world, to things visible and to things invisible. Christ is risen from the dead; rise with him. Christ has returned to himself; return. Christ is freed from the tomb; be freed from the bonds of sin. The gates of hades are opened, and death is destroyed, and the old Adam is put aside, and the new is fulfilled.[4] If anyone in Christ is a new creation,[5] be made new." He said these things, and those surrounding him gave praise in song, as indeed they also did before, when Christ was manifested to us through his birth here below: "Glory to God in the highest and on earth peace, good will among humankind."[6] With them I also say these things among you; and if

[1]Hab 2.1.
[2]Cf. Matt 28.3.
[3]Cf. Rev 19.17.
[4]Here "Adam" refers not to the first-created man but to a mode of human existence here and now, either the old fallen condition or the new life in Christ.
[5]2 Cor 5.17.
[6]Luke 2.14.

only I could also receive a voice of angelic rank, and it would resound to all the ends of the earth.

2 The Lord's Pascha, Pascha, and again I will say Pascha, to the honor of the Trinity. It is to us the feast of feasts and festival of festivals, as far exalted above all—not only those that are merely human and crawl on the ground but also those that are of Christ himself and are celebrated for him—as the sun is above the stars. Beautiful indeed yesterday were our splendid array and procession of lights, in which we were united both privately and publicly, almost every sort of people and every rank, lighting up the night with plentiful fires.[7] This is a symbol of the great light, both the heavenly light that makes fire signals from above, shining on the whole world in its own beauty, and equally the light above the heavens, in the angels—the first nature illumined after the First and springing from it—and equally in the Trinity, by which every light has been produced, divided off from the undivided light and honored. Yet today is more beautiful and more illustrious, inasmuch as yesterday's light was a forerunner of the great light's rising, and as it were a kind of pre-festal gladness. But today we celebrate the resurrection itself, not as still hoped for but as having already occurred and gathering the whole world to itself. Let different persons therefore bring forth different fruits for this occasion and bring festal gifts, either small or greater, of things spiritual and dear to God, as far as each has the power. For the gifts of angels, those first and intelligible and pure beings who behold and testify to the glory above, can scarcely attain the feast's rank, if indeed the whole song of praise is also accessible to them. But we will contribute a discourse, the most beautiful and most honorable thing we have, especially when singing the praises of the Word for a good deed done for reason-endowed nature.[8] I will begin from this

[7] Gregory is describing the Paschal Vigil.

[8] In this sentence Gregory brings together three meanings of the word *logos*: his "discourse," the divine "Word," and the rationality of "reason-endowed" (*logikes*) human nature.

point. For I cannot bear, when offering a sacrifice of words about the great sacrifice and the greatest of days, not to run back to God and from there make my beginning. And purify for me your mind and hearing and reasoning, all you who feast on such things—since the discourse is about God and things divine—that you may depart truly filled and not empty. But it will be at the same time very full and very concise, so as neither to distress you by its deficiency nor be unpleasant due to satiety.

3   God always was and is and will be, or rather always "is," for "was" and "will be" belong to our divided time and transitory nature; but he is always "he who is," and he gave himself this name when he consulted with Moses on the mountain.[9] For holding everything together in himself, he possesses being, neither beginning nor ending. He is like a kind of boundless and limitless sea of being, surpassing all thought and time and nature. He is sketched only by the mind, and this in a very indistinct and mediocre way, not from things pertaining to himself but from things around him. Impressions are gathered from here and there into one particular representation of the truth, which flees before it is grasped and escapes before it is understood. It illumines the directive faculty in us, when indeed we have been purified, and its appearance is like a swift bolt of lightning that does not remain. It seems to me that insofar as it is graspable, the divine draws [us] toward itself, for what is completely ungraspable is unhoped for and unsought. Yet one wonders at the ungraspable, and one desires more intensely the object of wonder, and being desired it purifies, and purifying it makes deiform, and with those who have become such he converses as with those close to him,—I speak with vehement boldness—God is united with gods,[10] and he is thus known, perhaps as much as he already knows those who are known to him.[11]

[9]Exod 3.14, LXX.
[10]Ps 82.1, 6.
[11]1 Cor 13.12.

For the divine is without limits and difficult to contemplate, and this alone is entirely graspable in it, namely that it is without limits, whether one supposes that to be a simple nature is to be wholly ungraspable or perfectly graspable. For what is a being whose nature is simple? Let us inquire further, for simplicity is clearly not the nature of this being, just as composition alone is clearly not the nature of composite entities.

4 The absence of limit is contemplated in two ways, with regard to the beginning and to the end, for that which is above both and is not contained between them is without limit. When the mind gazes steadfastly into the depth above, not having a place to stand and relying on the representations it has of God, from this perspective it names as "without beginning" that which is without limit and without outlet. Yet when it gazes at what is below and what is subsequent, it names it "immortal" and "indestructible"; and when it views the whole together, "eternal." For eternity is neither time nor some part of time, nor is it measurable, but what is time for us measured by the movement of the sun is for everlasting beings eternity, since it is coextensive with these beings, as if it were a kind of movement and interval of time.

For me this is enough philosophizing about God at present. For it is not the time to go beyond these things, since our concern here is not "theology" but "economy."[12] When I say "God," I mean Father and Son and Holy Spirit. The divinity is not diffused beyond these, lest we introduce a crowd of gods, but nor is it limited to fewer than these, lest we be condemned to a poverty of divinity, either Judaizing because of the monarchy or hellenizing because of the abundance. For the evil is alike in both cases, though it is found in opposites. This then is the Holy of Holies, which is veiled by the Seraphim and

[12]Among the Greek fathers, *theologia* often refers to discussion of God in Godself. The corresponding term *oikonomia* refers to discussion of God's relations to the created world, including the divine plan of salvation through the incarnation of Jesus Christ.

glorified with a threefold "Holy,"[13] converging in one Lordship and divinity, which another who preceded us has explained in a most beautiful and exalted way.

5 Yet it was not sufficient for goodness to be moved only in contemplation of itself, but it was necessary that the good be poured forth and given paths to travel, so that there would be more recipients of its benevolent activity, for this was the summit of goodness. Therefore it first thought of the angelic and heavenly powers, and the thought was action, accomplished by the Word and perfected by the Spirit. And thus were created the second splendors, the servants of the first Splendor, which are either intelligent spirits, or a kind of immaterial or bodiless fire, or some other nature as close to this as possible. I would like to say that they are unmoved toward evil and have only the movement toward the good, since they are around God and are the first to be illumined by God; for things here below are illumined second. Yet I am persuaded to consider and say that they are not immovable but only difficult to move on account of the one who was called Lucifer [i.e. Light-Bearer] because of his splendor[14] but both became and is called darkness because of his pride, and the rebellious powers under him, who are fashioners of evil through their flight from the good and incite evil in us.

6 So therefore for these reasons the intelligible world was created by God, at least as far as I can investigate these matters, estimating great things by my small discourse. And since the first world was beautiful to him, he thought a second material and visible world, that which is composed of heaven and earth and the system and composite of realities existing between them. It is praiseworthy because of the good disposition of each thing, but more praiseworthy because of the good connectedness and harmony of the whole, as each thing is well adapted to another and all to all, into the full realization of

[13]Isa 6.2–3.
[14]Isa 14.12–15.

one world. Thus God has shown that he was able to create not only a nature akin to himself but also what is entirely foreign to him. For the spiritual natures and those apprehended only by the mind are akin to the divine, but those apprehended by the senses are entirely foreign to it, and those which are entirely without life or movement are still farther removed.

7   Thus far mind and sense perception, distinguished from each other in this way, remained within their own limits and bore in themselves the magnificence of the Creator Word. They silently praised the greatness of his works and were heralds sounding afar.[15] But there was not yet a blending out of both, nor a mixing of opposites, which is the distinctive sign of a greater wisdom and of divine superabundance concerning created natures, nor was the full wealth of goodness yet made known. So then wishing to manifest this, the Creator Word also makes one living creature out of both, I mean invisible and visible natures, that is the human being. And having taken the body from the matter already created, he breathed in breath from himself,[16] which is surely the intelligent soul and the image of God of which Scripture speaks.[17] The human being is a kind of second world, great in smallness, placed on the earth, another angel, a composite worshiper, a beholder of the visible creation, an initiate into the intelligible, king of things on earth, subject to what is above, earthly and heavenly, transitory and immortal, visible and intelligible, a mean between greatness and lowliness. He is at once spirit and flesh, spirit on account of grace, flesh on account of pride, the one that he might remain and glorify his Benefactor, the other that he might suffer and in suffering remember and be corrected if he has ambition for greatness. He is a living creature trained here and transferred elsewhere, and, to perfect the mystery, deified through inclination toward God. For the light and the truth present in mea-

[15]Ps 19.3–4.
[16]Gen 2.7.
[17]Gen 1.26–27.

sure here bear me toward this end, to see and experience the splendor of God, which is worthy of the one who has bound me [to flesh] and will release me and hereafter will bind me in a higher manner.

8 This being was placed in paradise,[18] whatever that paradise was then, honored with self-determination so that the good would belong to the one who chose it no less than to the one who provided its seeds. The human being was a cultivator of immortal plants,[19] that is perhaps divine thoughts, both the simpler and the more complete. He was naked[20] because of his simplicity and life free from artifice and far from any covering or screen, for such a condition befitted the one who existed at the beginning. God gave him a law as material on which his free choice could work, and the law was a commandment indicating which plants he could possess and which one he was not to touch. And that was the tree of knowledge,[21] which was neither planted from the beginning in a evil way nor forbidden through envy—let the enemies of God not wag their tongues in that direction, nor imitate the serpent[22]—but it would be good if possessed at the right time. For the tree is contemplation, according to my own contemplation, which is only safe for those of perfect disposition to undertake; but it is not good for those who are still simpler and those greedy in their desire, just as adult food is not useful for those who are still tender and in need of milk.[23] But after the devil's envy and the woman's spiteful treatment, both what she underwent as more tender and what she set before [the man] as more persuasive—alas for my weakness, for that of the first father is mine!—he forgot the commandment given him and yielded to the bitter taste.[24] And at once he came to be banished from the tree of

[18]Gen 2.8–15.
[19]Gen 2.15.
[20]Gen 2.25.
[21]Gen 2.16–17.
[22]Gen 3.1–3.
[23]1 Cor 3.2, 1 Pet 2.2.
[24]Gen 3.6.

life[25] and from paradise[26] and from God because of the evil, and was clothed in the tunics of skin,[27] that is perhaps the more coarse and mortal and rebellious flesh, and for the first time he knew his own shame and hid from God.[28] He gained a certain advantage from this; death is also the cutting off of sin, that evil might not be immortal, so the punishment becomes love for humankind. For thus, I am persuaded, God punishes.

9 The human being was first educated[29] in many ways corresponding to the many sins that sprouted from the root of evil for different reasons and at different times; by word, law, prophets, benefits, threats, blows, floods, conflagrations, wars, victories, defeats; signs from heaven, signs from the air, from earth, from sea; unexpected changes in men, cities, nations; by all this God sought zealously to wipe out evil. At the end a stronger remedy was necessary for more dreadful diseases: murders of each other, adulteries, false oaths, lusts for men, and the last and first of all evils, idolatry and the transfer of worship from the Creator to creatures.[30] Since these things required a greater help, they also obtained something greater. It was the Word of God himself, the one who is before the ages, the invisible, the ungraspable, the incorporeal, the Principle from the Principle, the light[31] from the light, the source of life[32] and immortality, the imprint[33] of the archetypal beauty, the immutable seal,[34] the undistorted image,[35] the definition and explanation of his Father. He approaches his own image[36] and bears flesh because of my flesh and

[25]Gen 2.9, 3.24.
[26]Gen 3.23.
[27]Gen 3.21.
[28]Gen 3.7–8.
[29]Heb 12.6.
[30]Rom 1.25.
[31]John 8.12.
[32]John 1.4, 11.25.
[33]Heb 1.3.
[34]John 6.27.
[35]Col 1.15.
[36]Gen 1.26–27.

mingles himself with a rational soul because of my soul, purifying like by like. And in all things he becomes a human being, except sin.[37] He was conceived by the Virgin, who was purified beforehand in both soul and flesh by the Spirit,[38] for it was necessary that procreation be honored and that virginity be honored more. He comes forth, God with what he has assumed, one from two opposites, flesh and spirit, the one deifying and the other deified. O the new mixture! O the paradoxical blending! He who is[39] comes into being, and the uncreated is created, and the uncontained is contained, through the intervention of the rational soul, which mediates between the divinity and the coarseness of flesh. The one who makes rich[40] becomes poor;[41] he is made poor in my flesh, that I might be enriched through his divinity. The full one[42] empties himself;[43] for he empties himself of his own glory for a short time, that I may participate in his fullness. What is the wealth of his goodness? What is this mystery concerning me? I participated in the [divine] image,[44] and I did not keep it; he participates in my flesh both to save the image and to make the flesh immortal. He shares with us a second communion, much more paradoxical than the first; then he gave us a share in what is superior, now he shares in what is inferior. This is more godlike than the first; this, to those who can understand, is more exalted.

10 Yet perhaps one who is excessively ardent and devoted to feasts may ask, What are these things to us? Spur on your pony toward the goal post. Investigate for us what concerns the feast and the reasons why we are here today. Truly I will do this, even if I have begun with things a bit exalted, since my desire and my discourse have constrained me. But it probably does no harm to the lovers of learning

[37]Heb 4.15.
[38]Luke 1.35.
[39]Exod 3.14, LXX.
[40]Rom 10.12, 2 Cor 8.9.
[41]2 Cor 8.9.
[42]Col 2.9.
[43]Phil 2.7.
[44]Gen 1.26–27.

and beauty to discuss briefly the meaning of the word Pascha itself, for this addition might not prove trivial to their ears. This great and venerable Pascha is called "Phaska" by the Hebrews in their own language, and the word means "passing over": in the historical sense the flight and migration from Egypt to Canaan; and in the spiritual sense the progress and ascent from things below to things above and to the land of promise. And we have also observed here something we have found to occur in many texts of Scripture, the alteration of certain names from what is more obscure to what is clearer, or from what is cruder to what is more refined. For some, considering this word to be a name for the Savior's passion, then hellenizing the word by changing the *ph* to a *p* and the *k* to a *ch*, have called the day Pascha. And custom adopted the word and made it prevail, as it came to the ears of many as a more pious term.

11 So before our time the divine Apostle declared the law to be entirely a shadow of things to come and intelligible things.[45] For God also, who before this gave oracles to Moses, when he legislated about these things said, "See that you make all things according to the pattern shown you on the mountain."[46] He showed the visible things to be a kind of sketch and outline of the invisible things. And I am persuaded that there is nothing random, nothing irrational, nothing base among those things appointed, nothing unworthy of the legislation of God and the ministry of Moses, even if for each of the types it is difficult to discover a spiritual interpretation extending to each detail, of things legislated about the tabernacle itself and its measurements and materials, and the things carried by the Levites and priests, and of matters concerning sacrifices and purifications and offerings; and these are to be contemplated only by those like Moses in virtue, or very close to him in learning. For indeed on the mountain itself God appears to human beings, as he himself descends from his own height while leading us up from the lowliness

[45]Heb 10.1.
[46]Exod 25.40.

below, that the Incomprehensible may be comprehended at least in the measure possible and as far as is safe for mortal nature. For in no other way does the coarseness of a material body and a captive mind come to comprehension of God except by being helped. Then accordingly not all appear to be deemed worthy of the same rank and position, but one is worthy of this, another of that, each, in my opinion, according to the measure of his own purification; and others have been altogether excluded, and are only allowed to hear the voice from above, as many as are like beasts in character and unworthy of divine mysteries.

12   Yet as we move forward in the middle between those who are entirely coarse in mind and those who are too contemplative and exalted, that we may neither remain altogether idle and unmoved nor be busier than we ought and be banished and estranged from the prizes set before us—for the one is somehow Jewish and low, the other is dream interpretation, and both alike are condemned—we will discuss these matters, as far as is within our reach and is not very strange or ridiculous to the multitude. For we believe that since we had fallen due to sin from the beginning and been led away by plea-sure as far as idolatry and lawless bloodshed, we needed to be called back again and restored to our original state, through the heartfelt compassion of God our Father, who could not bear that such a work of his own hands as the human being[47] should be lost. How, then, were we to be formed anew, and what was to happen? A violent rem-edy was rejected as unpersuasive and capable of wounding because of our chronic pride, but a gentle and compassionate therapy was planned to set us right again. For a crooked branch will not bear to be suddenly bent the other way and forced by the hand straightening it, but it will be more quickly broken than set right; nor will a fiery horse above a certain age bear the tyranny of a bridle without some coaxing and encouraging sounds. For this reason the law is given us to help as a kind of middle wall between God and idols, leading us

[47]Gen 2.7.

away from them and restoring us to him. And it concedes a little at first so as to gain something greater. It concedes sacrifices for a while so as to establish God in us, that subsequently, at the right time, it may end sacrifices too, wisely changing us by gradual removals, and leading us to the gospel already trained for willing obedience.

13 In this way, then, and for these reasons, the written law was introduced, to draw us together into Christ, and this is the rationale for the sacrifices, according to my rationale. And that you may not be ignorant of the depth of God's wisdom and the wealth of his unsearchable judgments,[48] he did not leave these altogether unconsecrated or useless, or let them be offerings of mere blood. Rather, the offering, Christ, who is great and unsacrificed, if I may speak thus, in regard to his first nature,[49] has been intermingled with the sacrifices of the law and was a purification not for a small part of the inhabited earth or for a short time but for all the world and throughout the ages. For this reason a lamb is chosen[50] for its innocence and for the clothing of the original nakedness.[51] For such is the offering given for us, who both is and is called a robe of incorruption. And he is perfect,[52] not only because of his divinity—for nothing is more perfect than the divine—but also because of what was assumed,[53] which has been anointed with divinity and become that which anointed it, and, I make bold to say, one with God. And he is male[54] as offered for Adam, or rather the stronger for the strong, since the first man fell under sin, and most of all because he bears nothing female, nothing unmanly, in himself; but he cried out loudly[55] from

---

[48]Rom 11.33.
[49]That is, his divine nature.
[50]Exod 12.3ff.
[51]Gen 3.7.
[52]Exod 12.5.
[53]That is, his humanity.
[54]Exod 12.5.
[55]Browne and Swallow, in *NPNF*² 7:427, mistranslate ἐκραγὲν βίᾳ as "burst." It is rendered here as "cried out loudly." Gregory speaks of a baby's cry that is also the mighty voice of the divine Word sounding forth from within the womb where it has become

the virginal and maternal bonds with great power, and a male was born from the prophetess, as Isaiah proclaims the good news.[56] And he is one year old as the sun of righteousness,[57] starting from above, then circumscribed by that which is visible, then returning to himself. He is the blessed crown of goodness[58] and is in every way equal to himself and like himself, and not only this but also as giving life to the circle of the virtues, which are gently commingled and mixed with each other by a law of friendship and order. And he is without fault and guileless as the healer of faults and of the damage and defilement coming from evil. For though he both took upon himself our sins and carried away our diseases,[59] yet he himself has not suffered anything that called for healing. For he was tempted in everything like us but without sin.[60] For the one persecuting the light that shines in the darkness did not overcome it.[61]

14 What more? The first month is introduced, or rather the beginning of months.[62] Either this was so for the Hebrews from the beginning, or it became so later and because of the mystery and was taken as first. And it is the tenth of the month, for that is the most complete number, among units the first perfect unit and generating

incarnate. This is very different from the picture of a male child bursting to freedom from maternal confinement, an image whose connotations misrepresent Gregory and portray his understanding of Christ and his virgin Mother in a distorted way.

[56]Isa 8.3. Note that Christ's maleness here has an allegorical, not a literal or ontological significance. Gregory ascribes to him the attributes of the paschal lamb. In the next sentence he is said to be one year old, which could not have been literally true at the time of his passion.

[57]Mal 4.2.

[58]Ps 65.11, "You crown the year with your bounty." Here Gregory pictures the year as a circle, the shape of a wreath or crown. He also alludes to the Psalm, which speaks of God's bounty, perhaps originally the harvest, as crowning the year. Through this imagery, he speaks of Christ as embodying the fullness of all the virtues, which are joined to each other in a single circle. The idea that all the virtues are interconnected is a commonplace of classical philosophy and is important to Gregory of Nyssa.

[59]Isa 53.4ff.
[60]Heb 4.15.
[61]John 1.5.
[62]Exod 12.2ff.

perfection. And the lamb is kept until the fifth day, perhaps because my sacrifice purifies the senses, from which come falls, and around which there is war, since through them the goad of sin is taken into oneself. And it is selected not only from the lambs[63] but also from the worse species, from the young goats on the left hand,[64] because it is slain not only for the just but also for sinners; and maybe even more for them, since we also have a greater need for lovingkindness. And it is not surprising if the sheep is first of all sought for each household, but if this does not occur due to poverty then by contributions from the households belonging to a family. This is because it is best above all that each should himself suffice for his own perfecting and offer a living sacrifice holy to God who calls, consecrated always and in everything; but if not, then co-workers should be used in this who are kin and have a virtuous lifestyle. For to me this appears to be the meaning of sharing the sacrifice with those nearest if needed.

15 Then comes the holy night when the present life was poured forth, this equally balanced night,[65] in which the darkness at the first creation is dissolved, and everything comes into light and order and form, and the former disorder receives the order of a world.[66] Then we flee Egypt, the angry and pursuing sin, and Pharaoh the invisible tyrant, and the assigner of bitter work, packing for the move to the world above. And we are freed from the clay and the brick-making, the husks and slippery places of this fleshly state of existence that for most is all but dominated by husk-like reasonings. Then the lamb is slain, and practice and reason are sealed with the precious blood, that is habit and activity, the supports of our doors. I speak in truth of the movements and opinions of the mind rightly opened

[63]Exod 12.5.

[64]Matt 25.33.

[65]Gregory refers to the spring equinox and draws on a traditional belief that God created the world at this time of year.

[66]Gen 1.1–3. The Greek word for "world," κόσμος, has connotations of order and beauty as well as existence. Here Gregory contrasts the ordered universe God creates in Gen 1.2 with the darkness and chaos that precede it.

and closed to contemplation, since there is a certain measure even to comprehension. Then comes the final and most severe blow to the pursuers, in truth worthy of night, and Egypt laments the firstborn of its own reasonings and practices. Scripture also calls this the seed of the Chaldeans that is removed⁶⁷ and the Babylonian infants that are hammered with the stone and destroyed.⁶⁸ And all things are full of the shout and cry of the Egyptians, and at that time their destroyer withdraws from us through reverence and fear of the anointing. Then comes the removal of leaven for seven days⁶⁹—for this is the most mystical of numbers and corresponds to this world—the leaven of the old and bitter evil, not that which makes bread and is alive, that we may not provide for ourselves any Egyptian dough⁷⁰ or remnant of Pharisaical and ungodly teaching.⁷¹

16   So let them lament, but we will eat the lamb, toward evening⁷² because Christ's passion comes at the consummation of the ages, and since he shares the mystery with his disciples in the evening,⁷³ dissolving the darkness of sin. And it is not boiled but roasted,⁷⁴ that our word may have nothing unexamined, nothing watery, nothing easily dissolved, but be entirely firm and solid, and tested by purifying fire, and free from everything material or superfluous. And let us be helped by the good coals⁷⁵ from the one coming to cast fire on the earth⁷⁶ that kindle and purify our reason, which destroys wicked habits and hastens to the kindling. Whatever, then, are the meaty and nourishing parts of the word,⁷⁷ let them be eaten and consumed by

---

⁶⁷Jdt 5.6.
⁶⁸Ps 137.8–9.
⁶⁹Exod 12.19.
⁷⁰Exod 12.19.
⁷¹Matt 16.6.
⁷²Exod 12.18.
⁷³That is, he shares the Eucharist with them at the Last Supper.
⁷⁴Exod 12.9.
⁷⁵Isa 6.6.
⁷⁶Luke 12.49.
⁷⁷The rest of this paragraph uses eating the paschal lamb as an allegory to describe principles for interpreting Scripture and handling difficult biblical texts. It

the inner and hidden faculties of the mind[78] and given up to spiritual digestion, from head to feet, from the first contemplations about the divinity to the last reflections about the incarnation. And let us not carry anything away or leave it until morning,[79] because the majority of our mysteries are not carried out to those outside,[80] nor is there any purification beyond this night, and delay is not commendable for those who share in the word.[81] For as indeed it is good and dear to God for anger not to last all day[82] but to be dissolved before sunset, both chronologically and anagogically, for it is not safe for us if the Sun or Justice sets upon us when we are angered; so also such food must not remain through the night, nor be stored until the next day. But whatever is bony and inedible, and difficult for us to comprehend, let it not be broken,[83] that is badly interpreted and understood. For I need not say that nor, according to the narrative, was a bone of Jesus broken, though indeed the death of those crucified was hastened because of the sabbath.[84] Nor must it be torn off and thrown away, that the holy things may not be given to dogs and to evil ones who tear to pieces the word, as indeed the radiant pearl of the word is not to be given to pigs.[85] But let it be consumed by the fire with which the

is commonplace among the fathers to understand studying and meditating on the Word of God as an important way of receiving spiritual nourishment. There is thus a parallel between the Word and the Eucharist. This passage surely reflects Origen's influence on Gregory in matters of biblical interpretation.

[78]Exod 12.8.

[79]Exod 12.10.

[80]Gregory refers to the *disciplina arcana* that still exists in his time, the practice of keeping sacraments such as baptism and the Eucharist secret from unbelievers and catechumens.

[81]Here Gregory speaks briefly of baptism, alluding to themes he has discussed at length in Oration 40. He says there is no second baptism beyond the first, which is usually performed on the paschal night. He then notes that the delay so common in his time is not good for the catechumens, those who attend only the service of the Word.

[82]Eph 4.26.

[83]Exod 12.46.

[84]John 19.31–33. Gregory alludes to the parallel and intimate connection between the word of Scripture and the Word incarnate as Jesus Christ.

[85]Matt 7.6.

whole burnt offerings are also consumed, winnowed and preserved by the Spirit who searches and perceives all things, not destroyed by water, or scattered as indeed Moses scattered the calf's head that Israel carelessly made, as a reproach to their hardheartedness.[86]

17 Yet it would not be fitting to neglect the way of eating either, since neither did the law, which in the letter labored even as far as this in contemplation. For we consume the victim in haste, eating it with unleavened bread and bitter herbs, and with loins girded, and wearing sandals, and leaning on a staff[87] like an old person. It is with haste, that we may not suffer that which was forbidden to Lot[88] by the commandment, that we may not look around or stay anywhere around there but get safely to the mountain, not be included with the Sodomites in the strange fire, nor solidified into a pillar of salt by turning back[89] to what is worse, which indeed results from delay. And it is with bitter herbs[90] because life in accord with God is bitter and arduous, especially for beginners, and is more exalted than pleasures. For if indeed the new yoke is gentle and the burden light,[91] as you have heard, this is, however, because of the hope, and the reward that is much more abundant than the sufferings here. Since otherwise who would not say that the gospel is much more troublesome and painful than the law's regulations? For while the law prevents the completion of sins, we are accused even for their causes, as being almost the deeds. "Do not commit adultery," says the law;[92] but you must not lust[93] either, kindling the passion by curious and diligent looks. "Do not murder," it says;[94] but you must not return a blow[95]

---

[86]Exod 32.19ff.
[87]Exod 12.8, 11.
[88]Gen 19.17.
[89]Gen 19.24–26.
[90]Exod 12.8.
[91]Matt 11.30.
[92]Exod 20.14.
[93]Matt 5.28.
[94]Exod 20.13.
[95]Matt 5.39.

either but even hand yourself over to the hitter. How much more philosophical the gospel is than the law! "Do not swear falsely," the law says;[96] but you must not swear to begin with, neither a small nor a greater oath,[97] since an oath gives birth to a false oath. "Do not join house to house," it says, "and field to field,"[98] oppressing the poor, but you must put aside willingly even your just possessions and be stripped for the poor,[99] that you may easily take up the cross and be enriched by things unseen.

18 Let the loins[100] of the non-rational animals be loose and unbound,[101] for they do not have reason that rules over pleasures. I need not say that even they have a limit to natural movements. But as for you, let that which desires and neighs[102]—as divine Scripture says, ridiculing the passion's shame—be girded up by a belt and self-control, that you may eat the Pascha purely, mortifying your members that are upon the earth[103] and imitating the belt of John, the desert dweller and forerunner and great herald of the truth.[104] I also know another belt, I mean the military and manly one, for which the Euzonoi of Syria and certain Monozonoi are named.[105] About this one God also says in response to Job, "No, but gird up your loins like a man"[106] and give a manly answer. With this belt also divine David boasts that he is girded all around with power from God,[107] and refers to God himself as clothed and girded all around

[96]Lev 19.2, Num 30.2, Deut 23.21.

[97]Matt 5.34.

[98]Isa 5.8.

[99]Matt 19.21, Mark 10.21.

[100]Gregory and his audience presuppose that "loins" are a biblical euphemism for the male genitalia.

[101]Cf. Exod 12.11.

[102]Jer 5.8.

[103]Col 3.5.

[104]Matt 3.4.

[105]2 Kgs 5.2. In Greek "Euzonoi" means "well-girded," and "Monozonoi" means "once-girded."

[106]Job 38.3.

[107]Ps 18.32.

with power,[108] clearly against the ungodly. Yet some might like to see in this the abundance of his power, which has been as it were girded up so as to be manifested indirectly, just as also he clothes himself with light as with a garment.[109] For who will endure his unchecked power and light? I ask, what do loins and truth have in common? What is meant by holy Paul in the saying, "Stand therefore with your loins girded all around with truth"[110]? Perhaps that contemplation is to bind desire on all sides and not allow it to aim elsewhere. For that which wishes to be disposed lovingly toward one thing does not have the same impulse toward other pleasures.

19   As for the sandals, let one who is about to touch the holy ground trodden by God take them off, just as renowned Moses did on the mountain,[111] that he might bring nothing dead, nothing to come between God and the human. And likewise if any disciple is sent for the sake of the gospel, let him go philosophically and with nothing superfluous. Besides being penniless and without staff and with only one coat, he must even be barefoot too,[112] that the feet of those proclaiming the gospel of peace and of every other good may appear beautiful.[113] But let those fleeing Egypt and the things of Egypt put sandals on[114] in order to be safe especially from the scorpions and snakes that Egypt produces abundantly, so as not to be crippled by those that watch the heel,[115] on which we have been commanded to trample.[116] About the staff[117] and its hidden meaning, I hold the following. I know one to lean on and one that is pastoral and educational and corrects the reason-endowed sheep.

[108]Ps 93.1.
[109]Ps 104.2.
[110]Eph 6.14.
[111]Exod 3.5.
[112]Matt 10.9–10.
[113]Isa 52.7.
[114]Exod 12.11.
[115]Gen 3.15.
[116]Luke 10.19.
[117]Exod 12.11.

But now the law mandates for you the staff to lean on, lest perhaps you become forgetful in thought when you hear of the blood of God, and his passion, and his death, lest perhaps you waver in an ungodly manner when advocating for God. But without shame and without hesitation eat his body and drink his blood, if you have a desire for life, neither disbelieving the words about the flesh nor hindered by those about the passion. By leaning, stand firm and secure, in nothing shaken by the adversary, nor swept away by falsely persuasive arguments. Stand upon your high place, set your feet in the courts of Jerusalem,[118] lean on the Rock that your steps in accord with God may not be shaken.

20 What do you say? That it seemed good to him that you come out of Egypt, the iron furnace,[119] leave behind you the polytheism that is there, and be led by Moses and his legislation and generalship? I will propose something that is not my own, or rather is very much my own, if you contemplate spiritually. Borrow from the Egyptians silver and gold vessels;[120] travel with them; supply yourself with strangers' belongings, or rather with your own. Pay is owed to you for the slave labor and the brick-making. You also, be a little clever in demanding payment; steal well. You endured hard labor there, fighting the clay, this wretched and filthy body, building foreign and tottering cities, whose memory perishes utterly with a cry.[121] What? Do you come out at your own cost and without pay? What? Do you leave behind for the Egyptians and the adverse powers what they obtained in an evil way and will spend in an even worse way? It is not theirs. They have seized it as booty, stolen it from the one who says, "The silver is mine, and the gold is mine,"[122] and I give it to whom I will. Yesterday it was theirs, for it was granted them. Today the Master brings it and gives it to you to be used well and in a saving

[118]Ps 122.2.
[119]Deut 4.20.
[120]Exod 11.2, LXX.
[121]Ps 9.6.
[122]Hag 2.8.

manner. Let us acquire for ourselves friends through the Mammon of injustice,[123] that when we fail they may in return receive us at the time of judgment.

21 If any of you is a Rachel or a Leah, a patriarchal and great soul, steal the idols of your father, whatever you find,[124] not to keep but to destroy. And if you are a wise Israelite move them to the land of promise, and let the persecutor grieve over them and, being outwitted, know that it is futile to tyrannize and enslave his betters. If you do this and come out of Egypt in this way, I know well that you will be led by a pillar of fire and cloud night and day,[125] a desert will be tamed, a sea will be divided[126] for you. Pharaoh will be submerged,[127] bread will rain down,[128] a rock will become a spring.[129] Amalek will be completely subdued, not with weapons alone but also with the hostile hands of the righteous, forming together with prayer a type of the unconquerable trophy of the cross.[130] A river will be driven back,[131] the sun will stand still, the moon will be held back,[132] walls will be brought down even without siege engines,[133] wasps will go before you to make a way for Israel and keep back the foreign tribes.[134] And all the other things that are recounted after these and with these—not to lengthen the discourse unduly—will be given to you by God. Such is the feast you are celebrating today. May the birthday of the one born for you and the burial of the one who suffered for you be such a feast, may the mystery of Pascha be

[123]Luke 16.9.
[124]Gen 31.19.
[125]Exod 13.21.
[126]Exod 14.21.
[127]Exod 14.28.
[128]Exod 16.15.
[129]Exod 17.6.
[130]Exod 17.10–13.
[131]Josh 3.13–17.
[132]Josh 10.13.
[133]Josh 6.20.
[134]Josh 24.12.

such for you. These things the law sketched beforehand; these things Christ fulfilled, the dissolver of the letter, the perfecter of the Spirit, who by his passion teaches suffering and by his glorification grants glorification with himself.

22 Now then, we will examine an issue and doctrine overlooked by many but in my view very much to be examined. To whom was the blood poured out for us, and why was it poured out, that great and renowned blood of God, who is both high priest and victim? For we were held in bondage by the Evil One, sold under sin, and received pleasure in exchange for evil. But if the ransom is not given to anyone except the one holding us in bondage, I ask to whom this was paid, and for what cause? If to the Evil One, what an outrage! For the robber would receive not only a ransom from God, but God himself as a ransom, and a reward so greatly surpassing his own tyranny that for its sake he would rightly have spared us altogether. But if it was given to the Father, in the first place how? For we were not conquered by him. And secondly, on what principle would the blood of the Only-begotten delight the Father, who would not receive Isaac when he was offered by his father but switched the sacrifice, giving a ram in place of the reason-endowed victim?[135] It is clear that the Father accepts him, though he neither asked for this nor needed it, because of the divine plan, and because the human being must be sanctified by the humanity of God, that God might himself set us free and conquer the tyrant by force and lead us back to himself by the mediation of the Son, who also planned this to the honor of the Father, to whom it is manifest that he yields all things. This much we have said of Christ, and the greater part will be revered by silence. But the bronze serpent is hung up to oppose the biting serpents[136] not as a representation[137] of the one who suffered for us but as a contrast.[138] It saves those who look at it not because they

[135]Gen 22.10–13.
[136]Num 21.9.
[137]Literally, "a type."
[138]Literally, "an antitype."

believe it is alive but because it has been killed and kills with itself the powers subject to it, being destroyed as indeed it deserved. And what is a fitting funeral oration for it from us? "Death, where is your sting? Hades, where is your victory?"[139] By the cross you have been overthrown, by the giver of life you have been put to death. You are without breath, dead, motionless, without activity, even if you keep the form of a serpent lifted high on a pole.

23 Now we will participate in a Pascha that is still a type even if more clearly unveiled than the old one, for the Pascha under the law, I boldly declare, was a more indistinct type of a type. But a little later, our participation will be more perfect and more pure; when the Word drinks anew with us in the kingdom of the Father,[140] he will reveal and teach that which now he has shown in a limited way. For what is now made known is ever new. And a certain drinking and enjoyment is ours to learn, but it is his to teach and to share the word with his disciples. For the teaching is nourishment, even for the nourisher.[141] But come, let us also partake of the law, in the manner of the gospel but not the letter, perfectly but not imperfectly, eternally but not temporarily. Let us make our head not the Jerusalem below but the city above,[142] not what is now trampled by soldiers[143] as a campground but what is glorified by angels. Let us not sacrifice a young calf, or a lamb that grows horns and hooves[144] in which much is dead and without sensation, but let us sacrifice to God a sacrifice of praise[145] on the altar above with the choirs on high. Let us pass through the first veil, let us approach the second, let us peep into the Holy of Holies.[146] Yet I will tell you something greater: let

[139]1 Cor 15.55.
[140]Matt 26.29.
[141]John 4.34.
[142]Heb 12.22.
[143]Luke 21.20–24.
[144]Ps 69.31.
[145]Heb 13.15.
[146]Heb 10.20.

us sacrifice ourselves to God, or rather offer sacrifice every day and in every movement. Let us accept all things for the Word. By sufferings let us imitate his suffering, by blood let us exalt his blood, let us willingly climb up on the cross. Sweet are the nails, even if very painful. For to suffer with Christ and for Christ is preferable to feasting with others.

24   If you are Simon of Cyrene, take up the cross and follow.[147] If you are crucified with him as a thief,[148] come to know God as kindhearted; if he was counted among the lawless because of you and your sin,[149] become law abiding because of him. Worship the one hanged for you even if you are hanging; gain something even from the evil, purchase salvation by death. Come into paradise[150] with Jesus so as to learn from what you have fallen. Contemplate the beauties there; leave the murmurer to die outside with his blasphemies. And if you are Joseph from Arimathea,[151] ask for the body from the crucifier; let that which cleanses the world[152] become yours. And if you are Nicodemus, the nocturnal worshipper of God, bury him with scented ointments.[153] And if you are a certain Mary or another Mary or Salome or Joanna, weep at daybreak. Be first to see the stone removed,[154] and perhaps the angels and Jesus himself. Say something, hear his voice. If you hear, "Do not touch me,"[155] stand far off, have reverence for the Word, but do not be sorrowful. For he knows those by whom he was seen first. Keep the feast of the resurrection; help Eve, the first who fell, and her who first greeted Christ and made him known to the disciples.[156] Become Peter or John; hasten to the

---

[147] Matt 27.32, Mark 15.21.
[148] Luke 23.40–43.
[149] Isa 53.11–12.
[150] Luke 23.43.
[151] Luke 23.50–53.
[152] 1 John 1.7.
[153] John 19.39.
[154] Mark 16.1–4.
[155] John 20.17.
[156] Browne and Swallow's translation, *NPNF*² 7:432, portrays this unnamed

tomb, running against each other, running together,[157] competing in the good competition. And if you are beaten in speed, win in zeal, not just peeping into the tomb but going inside. And if like Thomas you are left behind when the disciples have assembled to whom Christ manifests himself, when you see[158] do not disbelieve; and if you disbelieve, believe those who tell you. If you cannot believe then either, believe the prints of the nails.[159] And if he descends into Hades,[160] go down with him. Know also the mysteries of Christ there: what is the saving plan, what is the reason for the twofold descent, to save everyone absolutely by his manifestation, or there also only those who believe.[161]

25 And if he ascends into heaven,[162] go up with him. Join with the angels escorting him or those receiving him. Give orders that the gates be lifted up[163] or become higher, that they may receive him, lifted high from his passion. To those in doubt because of the body and the identifying marks of the passion, with which he did not descend but did ascend, who because of this inquire, "Who is this King of glory?" answer that he is "the Lord strong and mighty,"[164] both in everything that he has always done and is doing and in the present battle and triumph of his humanity. Give to the question's double-mindedness this twofold answer. And suppose they marvel, asking as in Isaiah's drama, "Who is this arriving from Edom"[165] and from earthly things? Or how are the clothes of the one without blood or body red, as of one who treads a wine vat and tramples a full vat?

woman as the Mother of God. The context points rather to Mary Magdalene, who was first to encounter and greet the Risen Lord.

[157]John 20.2–4.
[158]John 20.24–25.
[159]John 20.27–28.
[160]1 Pet 3.19.
[161]Cf. Oration 40.36 and the note at the paragraph's end.
[162]Luke 24.51.
[163]Ps 24.7, 9.
[164]Ps 24.8.
[165]Isa 63.1ff.

Set forth the beauty of the raiment of the body that has suffered, adorned by the passion and made radiant by the divinity; nothing is more beloved or more beautiful than this.

26 In regard to these things,[166] what do the slanderers say to us, the bitter calculators of divinity, the accusers of praiseworthy things, the dark ones speaking of the light, the uneducated speaking of wisdom, for whom "Christ died in vain,"[167] the unthankful creatures, fashioned by the Evil One? Do you bring as a charge against God his good deed? Is he small because he is humble for your sake? Do you accuse the Good Shepherd because he went to the one who strayed,[168] he who laid down his life for the sheep,[169] to find the stray "on the mountains and the hills where you offered sacrifice,"[170] and having found it took it on his shoulder,[171] on which also he carried the cross, and having taken it brought it back to the life on high, and having brought it on high counted it again among those who remained there? Do you accuse him because he lit a lamp, his own flesh, and swept the house, cleansing the world of sin, and searched for the coin,[172] the royal image covered with a heap of passions, then calls together his friends,[173] the angelic powers, once he has found the coin, and makes participants in his joy those angels initiated into the mystery of his saving plan?[174] Do you accuse him because the most radiant Light follows the lamp, his forerunner John,[175] and the Word follows the voice,[176] and the Bridegroom follows the friend of

---

[166]Paragraphs 26–27 repeat Oration 38.14–15 word for word. Gregory again reuses old material in a new context.
[167]Gal 2.21.
[168]Luke 15.4.
[169]John 10.11.
[170]Hos 4.13.
[171]Luke 15.5.
[172]Luke 15.8.
[173]Luke 15.9.
[174]Luke 15.8–9.
[175]John 5.35.
[176]John 1.23.

the bridegroom,[177] who prepares for the Lord a chosen people[178] and through water purifies them beforehand for the Spirit? Do you bring these charges against God? Do you also suppose that he is inferior for these reasons, that he girds himself with a towel and washes the feet of his disciples,[179] and shows that the best way to be exalted is lowliness,[180] since he lowers himself because of the soul bent down to the ground,[181] so as also to lift up with himself those leaning downward because of sin? But how do you not accuse him because he also eats with tax collectors and at the homes of tax collectors[182] and makes tax collectors his disciples,[183] that he also may make some profit for himself? What profit? The salvation of sinners. If so, one must also blame the physician for bending over one who is ill and enduring the stench to give health to the sick; or one who through compassion leans over a pit to rescue, according to the law,[184] the animal that has fallen into it.

27 He was sent,[185] but as human, for he was twofold. For he was tired[186] and hungry[187] and thirsty[188] and endured agony[189] and wept[190] through the law of the body, but if he underwent these things also as God, what of it? Consider the good will of the Father to be sent forth, and to it the Son ascribes his own activities, both as honoring the timeless Beginning and so as not to seem to be a

[177]Matt 3.11, 9.15; Luke 3.16, 5.34–35; John 1.26.
[178]Luke 1.17, Tit 2.14.
[179]John 13.4.
[180]Luke 14.11, 18.14.
[181]Matt 26.38–39, Mark 14.34–35.
[182]Matt 9.11, Luke 19.2, 7.
[183]Matt 9.9, Mark 2.14, Luke 5.27–28.
[184]Deut 22.4.
[185]John 3.34, 5.36–37, 6.40, etc.
[186]John 4.6.
[187]Matt 4.2, 21.18.
[188]John 4.7, 19.28.
[189]Luke 22.49.
[190]Luke 19.41, John 11.35.

rival god. For indeed Scripture says that he was given up,[191] but it is also written that he gave himself up;[192] and he was raised and taken up to heaven by the Father,[193] but he also resurrected himself and ascended there again.[194] For one is the Father's good will, the other is his own power. You speak of what belittles him, but you overlook what exalts him; you recognize that he suffered, but you do not add that it was voluntary. It is as if the Word still suffers now! By some he is honored as God but confused with the Father; by others he is dishonored as flesh and separated from him. Against which is one more angry? Rather, whom must one pardon more? Those who unite Father and Son wrongly or those who divide them? For the former would need to distinguish and the latter would need to conjoin; the ones in regard to number, the others in regard to divinity. Do you take offense at the flesh? So did the Jews. Do you also call him a Samaritan ?[195] I will be silent about the rest. Do you disbelieve in his divinity? This even the demons do not do.[196] O you who are more unbelieving than demons and more senseless than Jews! The latter regarded "Son" as a term denoting equality of honor,[197] the former knew that God drove them out,[198] for they were persuaded by what they suffered. But you neither accept the equality nor confess the divinity. It would have been better for you to be circumcised and possessed by a demon, if I may say something ridiculous, rather than in uncircumcision and good health to be in a state of wickedness and atheism. But let the war against these heretics be ended, at least if they finally want to come to their senses, or let it be postponed if they do not make this choice but continue as they are. But in any case we will fear nothing when struggling on behalf of the Trinity together with the Trinity.

[191] Rom 4.25, 1 Cor 11.23.
[192] Gal 2.20, Eph 5.2, 25.
[193] Acts 17.31, Rom 4.24, Mark 16.19.
[194] Matt 22.6, Mark 16.9, 19.
[195] John 8.48.
[196] Jas 2.9.
[197] John 5.18.
[198] Mark 1.34, Luke 4.41.

28 Now we must sum up the discourse as follows. We came into being that we might enjoy good things; we enjoyed good things when we came into being. We were entrusted with paradise that we might feast abundantly. We received a commandment, that we might be of good repute by keeping it, though God was not ignorant of what would happen but legislated self-determination. We were deceived since we were envied; we were driven out since we transgressed. We then fasted since before we did not fast, being overcome by the tree of knowledge. For the commandment was old; it came into existence at the same time as us and reasonably enjoined on us a kind of education for the soul and restraint of feasting, so that what we threw away by not keeping it we might recover by keeping it. We needed a God made flesh and made dead, that we might live. We were made dead with him that we might be purified. We have risen with him since we were made dead with him. We were glorified with him since we rose with him.

29 Many indeed are the wonders of that time: God crucified; the sun darkened and again rekindled, for created things also had to suffer with the Creator; the veil split; blood and water pouring from his side, the first as human, the second as above the human; the earth shaken, rocks broken in pieces for the sake of the Rock; dead people raised to bring faith in the completion of the universal resurrection; the signs at the tomb and after the tomb. Who can adequately sing their praise? Yet none is like the wonder of my salvation: a few drops of blood recreate the whole world and become for all human beings like a curdling agent for milk, binding and drawing us together into one.

30 But, O Pascha, great and holy and purifier of all the world, I will speak to you as to a living being.[199] O Word of God and light and life and wisdom and power! For I rejoice in all your names. O

[199] As the rest of this paragraph shows, the Pascha to which Gregory refers here is Christ himself.

offspring and movement and imprint of the Great Mind! Apprehended as Word and contemplated as human, you uphold all things, binding them by the word of your power! Accept now this discourse, not as firstfruits but perhaps as a completion of the fruit we offer, as a thank-offering and at the same time a supplication, that we may suffer nothing beyond the necessary and sacred things pertaining to us; and stop the body's tyranny over us—you see, Lord, how great it is and how burdensome; or what you decree, if we are to be purified by you. But if we are to be released worthily as we desire, and received in the heavenly tabernacle, perhaps also there we will make acceptable offerings to you on your holy altar, O Father and Word and Holy Spirit, for to you belong all glory, honor and sovereignty, to the ages of ages. Amen.

Gregory's Orations Read Liturgically in the Byzantine Church

George Galavaris, in *The Illustrations of the Liturgical Homilies of Gregory Nazianzenus*,[1] has shown that according to Byzantine manuscripts that follow the church calendar, sixteen orations were appointed to be read liturgically from the ninth century onward. The sequence of homilies varies in different manuscripts, but the most common usage is as follows.

Oration 1	*On Pascha and on His Slowness*	Pascha
Oration 45	*On Pascha*	Monday of Bright Week
Oration 44	*On New Sunday*	First Sunday after Pascha (Thomas Sunday)
Oration 41	*On Pentecost*	Pentecost
Oration 15	*On the Maccabees*	August 1, Feast of the Maccabees
Oration 24	*On the Holy Hieromartyr Cyprian*	October 2, Feast of St Cyprian

[1]George Galavaris, *The Illustrations of the Liturgical Homilies of Gregory Nazianzenus* (Princeton, NJ: Princeton University Press, 1969), 6–17.

Oration 19	*On his Orations and to the Tax Assessor Julian*	December 21, when Matt 18.21–36 is read, a parable about creditors and debtors
Oration 38	*On the Nativity of Christ*	December 25, Feast of the Nativity of Christ
Oration 43	*On the Great Basil*	January 1, Feast of St Basil the Great
Oration 39	*On Theophany*	January 6, Feast of Theophany (Epiphany)
Oration 40	*On Baptism*	January 7, Feast of St John the Baptist
Oration 11	*To Gregory of Nyssa, the Brother of Basil the Great*	January 10, Feast of St Gregory of Nyssa
Oration 21	*On the Great Athanasius*	January 18, Feast of St Athanasius the Great
Oration 42	*Farewell Address*	January 25, Feast of St Gregory of Nazianzus (the Theologian)
Oration 14	*On Love of the Poor*	Sunday of the Last Judgment. Gospel reading: Matt 25.31–46
Oration 16	*On his Father's Silence about the Plague of Hail*	Forgiveness Sunday. Gospel reading: Matt 6.14–21

Select Bibliography

Texts

Bernardi, J., ed. *Grégoire de Nazianze: Discours 1–3.* Sources chrétiennes 247. Paris: Editions du Cerf, 1978.

Calvet-Sebasti, M.-A., ed. *Grégoire de Nanianze: Discours 6–12.* Sources chrétiennes 405. Paris: Editions du Cerf, 1995.

Gallay, P., ed. *Grégoire de Nazianze: Discours 27–31 (Discours théologiques).* Sources chrétiennes 250. Paris: Editions du Cerf, 1978.

Migne, J.P., ed. Patrologia graeca [= Patrologiae cursus completus: Series graeca]. 162 vols. Paris, 1857–1886. 36:625–664.

Moreschini, C., ed. *Grégoire de Nazianze: Discours 38–41.* Sources chrétiennes 358. Paris: Editions du Cerf, 1990.

Translations

Browne, C.E., and J.E. Swallow, eds. and trans. *St Gregory Nazianzen: Select Orations.* Fathers of the Church, Ser. 2, Vol. 7. Grand Rapids, MI: Eerdmans, 1983. [Reprint]

Daley, B.E., S.J., ed. and trans. *Gregory of Nazianzus.* The Early Church Fathers. Abingdon, Oxfordshire and New York: Routledge, 2006.

Gilbert, P., ed. and trans. *On God and Man: The Theological Poetry of St Gregory of Nazianzus.* Crestwood, NY: SVS Press, 2001.

Meehan, D., ed. and trans. *St Gregory of Nazianzus: Three Poems*, Fathers of the Church 75. Washington, DC: Catholic University of America Press, 1987.

Moreschini, C., and D.A. Sykes, eds. and trans. *Gregory of Nazianzus: Poemata Arcana.* Oxford: Oxford University Press, 1996.

Vinson, M., ed. and trans., *St Gregory of Nazianzus: Select Orations*. Fathers of the Church 107. Washington, DC: Catholic University of America Press, 2003.

White, C., ed. and trans. *Gregory of Nazianzus: Autobiographical Poems*. Cambridge: Cambridge University Press, 1996.

Williams, F., and L. Wickham, trans. *St Gregory of Nazianzus: The Five Theological Orations and Two Letters to Cledonius*. Crestwood, NY: SVS Press, 2002.

Studies

Alfeyev, H. *Le chantre de la lumière: Introduction à la spiritualité de saint Grégoire de Nazianze*. Paris: Editions du Cerf, 2006.

Beeley, C. *Gregory of Nazianzus on the Trinity and the Knowledge of God*. Oxford and New York: Oxford University Press, 2008.

Børtnes, J., and T. Hägg, eds. *Gregory of Nazianzus: Images and Reflections*. Copenhagen: Museum Tusculanum Press, 2006.

Galavaris, G. *The Illustrations of the Liturgical Homilies of Gregory Nazianzenus*. Princeton, NJ: Princeton University Press, 1969.

Harrison, N.V. "Translating Gregory of Nazianzus." *St Vladimir's Theological Quarterly* 51 (2007): 123–31.

Kennedy, G.A. *Greek Rhetoric under Christian Emperors*. Princeton, NJ: Princeton University Press, 1983.

McGuckin, J.A. *Saint Gregory of Nazianzus: An Intellectual Biography*. Crestwood, NY: SVS Press, 2001.

Young, F.M. "Panegyric and the Bible." *Studia Patristica* 25 (1993): 194–208.

Affordably priced classics by the Fathers of the Church
From St Vladimir's Seminary Press

ST GREGORY OF NAZIANZUS
On God and Christ
The Five Theological Orations and Two Letters to Cledonius

ST GREGORY OF NAZIANZUS
*The Five Theological Orations
and Two Letters to Cledonius*

*Translation and Introduction
by Frederick Williams
and Lionel Wickham*

Gregory of Nazianzus, "The Theologian," was recognized among the Cappadocian Fathers as a vivid and quotable exponent of the doctrine of God in Trinity. These five sermons, probably delivered at the Chapel of the Resurrection in Constantinople, where Gregory was the bishop, contain his penetrating teaching. The English translation aims to capture for the present-day reader something of the atmosphere of intellectual excitement and spiritual exhilaration experienced by his first listeners. In addition, this work contains a new translation of Gregory's letters to Cledonius, which contain more focused reflections on the person of Jesus Christ, laying the groundwork for later Christology.

ISBN 978-0-88141-240-6 • 144 pp • Price: US $17.00

to order call 1-800-204-2665 or online at www.svspress.com

POPULAR PATRISTICS SERIES

ST VLADIMIR'S SEMINARY PRESS
1-800-204-2665 • www.svspress.com

We hope this book has been enjoyable and edifying for your spiritual journey toward our Lord and Savior Jesus Christ.

One hundred percent of the net proceeds of all SVS Press sales directly support the mission of St Vladimir's Orthodox Theological Seminary to train priests, lay leaders, and scholars to be active apologists of the Orthodox Christian Faith. However, the proceeds only partially cover the operational costs of St Vladimir's Seminary. To meet our annual budget, we rely on the generosity of donors who are passionate about providing theological education and spiritual formation to the next generation of ordained and lay servant leaders in the Orthodox Church.

Donations are tax-deductible and can be made at
www.svots.edu/give.
We greatly appreciate your generosity.

To engage more with St Vladimir's Orthodox
Theological Seminary, please visit:

www.svots.edu
online.svots.edu
www.svspress.com
www.instituteofsacredarts.com